THAT THE WORLD MAY BELIEVE

ALBERT C. OUTLER

A STUDY OF CHRISTIAN UNITY

Albert C. Outler

tHAT tHE WORLD
MAY BELIEVE

A STUDY OF CHRISTIAN UNITY

JOINT COMMISSION ON EDUCATION AND CULTIVATION

BOARD OF MISSIONS OF THE METHODIST CHURCH

475 Riverside Drive
New York, N. Y. 10027

LIBRARY OF CONGRESS CATALOG CARD NO. 66-13569

COVER AND FORMAT: Mamie Harmon

'The old order changeth, yielding place
　　　to new,
And God fulfills himself in many ways,
Lest one good custom should corrupt the
　　　world.
. . . More things are wrought by prayer
Than this world dreams of. Wherefore, let
　　　thy voice
Rise like a fountain . . . night and day.
For what are men better than sheep or goats
That nourish a blind life within the brain,
If, knowing God, they lift not hands
　　　of prayer
Both for themselves and those who call
　　　them friend?
For so the whole round earth is every way
Bound by gold chains about the feet of
　　　God. . . .'

Tennyson
from "Morte d'Arthur"

CONTENTS

RECOMMENDED MATERIALS

[1] Service Center, Board of Missions, The Methodist Church, 7820 Reading Road, Cincinnati, Ohio 45237.

* Forward Movement Publications, 412 Sycamore Street, Cincinnati, Ohio 45202. Single copies 25 cents; 10 copies to one address 20 cents each; 100 copies to one address 15 cents each.

† World Council of Churches, 475 Riverside Drive, New York, N. Y. 10027.

*COCU [Consultation on Church Union] by James W. Kennedy. Cincinnati: Forward Movement Publications, 1965. 25 cents

[1] COOPERATION OF MEN AND WOMEN IN CHURCH, FAMILY, AND SOCIETY by Madeleine Barot. Geneva: World Council of Churches, 1964. Paper, $1.00

Filmstrips: A FOUNDATION FOR DIALOGUE. A survey of the major Christian denominations in contemporary America. This initial understanding of the life, faith, and worship of other Christians provides a sound basis for positive thinking in the area of ecumenism and Christian dialogue. Two filmstrips with 209 frames, 43 minutes, color, 33⅓ rpm record. Order from the Convent of St. Catherine, Racine, Wisc. 53402. $8.50

*GOD'S CHURCH — NOT OURS by Paul Carlson. Cincinnati: Forward Movement Publications, 1965. 25 cents

†A GUIDE TO CHRISTIAN UNITY, Rev. ed., by George L. Hunt. St. Louis, Mo.: The Bethany Press, 1963.
Paper, $1.25

[1] HANDBOOK OF THE WORLD FEDERATION OF METHODIST WOMEN. Service Center. 50 cents

[1] LIVING ROOM DIALOGUES edited by William B. Greenspun, C.S.P. and William A. Norgren. New York: Paulist Press and the National Council of the Churches of Christ in the U.S.A., 1965. Order from the National Council of Churches, 475 Riverside Drive, New York, N. Y. 10027.   Paper, $1.00

[1] UNITED NATIONS AND WOMEN. World Federation of Methodist Women. Study Guide by Margaret Bender.
25 cents

[1] WHERE WE ARE IN CHURCH UNION edited by George L. Hunt and Paul A. Crow, Jr. New York: Association Press, 1965.   Paper, 75 cents

[Your attention is called to the "Glossary" (p. 191) which provides simple interpretations of some unfamiliar words as they are used in this study. We also call attention to "Books on Ecumenicity" (p. 181) which provides a wealth of information on the material now in existence. Ed.]

PREFACE

It is only fair that "the gentle reader" of this book be forewarned that its author is an ardent and unembarrassed advocate of Christian unity, grown old in the service of the ecumenical cause in one capacity or another, within his own church and in various councils of churches, local, state, national, world. Moreover, as one of the "delegated-observers" from the World Methodist Council to the Second Vatican Council, he has had the privilege of seeing, at first hand, the remarkable development of new ecumenical interests within the Roman Catholic Church, and between Catholics and Protestants at many levels. These experiences have, naturally, shaped the viewpoint reflected in these pages. The core conviction presented here is that Christian unity is an urgent divine imperative—and the most hopeful frontier in contemporary church life. How far this bias amounts to special pleading readers with other biases may judge.

But there are two disclaimers that may be entered here for the sake of clarity and candor. The first is that my zeal for ecumenism has little to do with that cozy feeling that delights in "Christian fellowship" for its own sake. The only valid warrant for such obvious risks and difficulties as are involved is that *unity is in order to mission—united witness* in the *world, united service* to the *world,* "that the world may come to believe" (John 17:21, author's translation).

The second disavowal would be unnecessary were it not

for the prejudice still abroad that unity inevitably means the swallowing of the scattered fragments of Christendom by the ecumenical leviathan—the loss of identity of our several traditions in one bloated superchurch, over-burdened by bigness, bustle, bureaucrats and bishops! But again, it is axiomatic in modern ecumenism that the recomposition of unity aims at the *fullness* of Christian community, and this can scarcely mean a single pattern of church life imposed upon all. The Christian family is incurably diverse: this is one of the plainest lessons of church history. But because of its common confession of Jesus Christ as Lord and Savior, it also aspires to be a genuine comm*unity*. Thus, the goal of true ecumenism is unity-in-creative-diversity and a natural diversity that lives gracefully within the compass of authentic unity. This, then, is the theme of these pages.

ALBERT C. OUTLER

CHAPTER ONE

THE SCANDAL
OF CHRISTIANS
IN DISUNITY

IN THE *Book of Common Prayer* and the new Methodist *Book of Worship for Church and Home* there is a collect "For the Unity of God's People" which is used occasionally in Methodist services and even more frequently in various kinds of interdenominational gatherings:

> O God, the Father of our Lord Jesus Christ our only Savior, the Prince of Peace: Give us grace seriously to lay to heart the great dangers we are in by *our unhappy divisions.* Take away all hatred and prejudice, and whatsoever else may hinder us from godly union and concord: that as there is but one Body and one Spirit, and one hope of our calling, one Lord, one Faith, one Baptism, one God and Father of us all, so we may be all of one heart and of one soul, united in one holy bond of truth and peace, of faith and charity, and may with one mind and one mouth *glorify thee;* through Jesus Christ our Lord. Amen.[1]

This is a good prayer, and an ancient one; it dates back to the fourth century and to the Liturgy of St. James.

[1] *The Book of Worship for Church and Home* (Nashville: The Methodist Publishing House, 1965), No. 3, p. 87. [Italics added by author.]

But in the places where I have been, the people who prayed it did not seem to feel that our divisions are really so "unhappy," after all. And this is not very strange, when one stops to think that the society in which we and our forebears have lived all our lives is radically pluralistic and that churches are always affected by their environment. It seems natural, in such a society, that all sorts of voluntary associations—social clubs, service clubs, labor unions, professional societies *and* churches—should spring up and then either flourish or falter depending on how they serve the needs and interests of their members. All too many people have come to think of the church as just another voluntary association, not only in their choice of a local congregation but in their relation to the church as a universal religious community. And since people's tastes in churches and churchmanship differ so widely, it seems self-evident to them that there ought to be as many different kinds of churches as there are "like-minded people." All of us know people who are firmly convinced that the divisions of the Christian community are actually happy, since they foster friendly competition and prevent any one of the churches from swallowing up the others. Our healthy fear of business monopoly has carried over into our notions about the church—and readily enough —since it is easier to think of organized religion as a kind of business than to discern in it "the pilgrim people of God on earth." Christian unity, so the argument goes, would necessarily be monopolistic and therefore would inevitably be dictatorial. And yet we know that it is of the essence of the gospel for faith to be free—that persons ought not to be coerced in their belief or unbelief. From this undoubted premise, the denominationalists draw a

3

doubtful conclusion: that the only kind of Christian unity that could exist would be in a monopolistic super-church, in which, obviously, this precious liberty of faith would be in jeopardy. Dr. Wayne Dehoney, president of the Southern Baptist Convention (1965-66), put this point for his tradition (denomination) in words that can be matched by those from other ardent denominationalists—Methodists, Lutherans, etc.:

> A second reason [why we have not been identified with the ecumenical movement] is that Southern Baptists generally are strong *denominationalists*. We do not accept the ecumenical premise that denominationalism is the scandal of Christianity, wasteful, selfish, or sinful. The variety of churches produced by the Protestant Reformation has brought great vitality and strength to Christianity. Division has multiplied the Christian witness. Struggle, tension, and doctrinal debate have purified truth and have been beneficial rather than harmful. To abolish denominationalism would be to reverse the Reformation and turn the clock back to a medieval Catholicism.[2]

No wonder, then, that many devout Christians are unmoved by, or else suspicious of, all the current talk about ecumenism. They are fearful of conformism in religion, jealous for the rights of the minorities and the nonconformists, aware of the values of creative dissent. Moreover, they are familiar with, and comfortable in, the traditions of denominationalism, and there are many who believe that denominationalism is God's providential arrangement for giving the Christian faithful a suitable range

2 Wayne Dehoney, "Southern Baptists and Ecumenical Concerns," *Christianity Today*, IX, No. 9 (January 29, 1965), 15.

of choice—in liturgy, theology, polity, and also in congenial social, racial, and business contacts as well. Denominationalism puts rival churches on their mettle to compete for God and glory and to provide their clienteles with what they want and are willing to pay for. It encourages like-minded folk to gravitate together; it reinforces the pleasures of coziness; and it provides outlets for both group leadership and group service. Moreover, it makes for a modicum of toleration of other expressions of religious faith and practice.

We are, therefore, accustomed to Christians in disunity and we have long ago salved our consciences (if they ever troubled us) on this point, since most of us have grown past the point of active enmity toward our "separated brethren." There is, of course, a great deal of prejudice left, based on the unsympathetic stereotypes that survive from our ancient quarrels. But the fact is that we really know little or nothing about these other Christians, and it seems that some of us couldn't care less.

And so we have gone on, untroubled by the divisions between the churches and unaware of the fact that our disunity is a stone of stumbling for the unbeliever who hears our proclamation—"one Lord, one Faith, one Baptism"—and disbelieves it because our sectarian actions obviously contradict our fine words. And yet, it was twenty-eight years ago, on the eve of Methodist union, that a great Methodist Protestant leader, Dr. James H. Straughn, put this point with painful clarity:

> If the Christian world cannot discover ways of ending its multitudinous strife, possessing as we are supposed to do a gospel of love toward God and all men and living under the

constant assurance of available heavenly resources of untold and unsuspected extent, if we cannot find ways of ending strife among ourselves it ill behooves us to chide governments and rulers and armies and navies for war and misery and crime and endless suffering. We bring to naught our suave assertions. Why should any agency believe the Christian ethic possesses healing for the strife of the nations and should employ our code when we have failed to exercise that gift among ourselves? Why should anyone believe that Christ is the hope of the world when the Church, his own broken, hurt body, cannot heal its own wounds?[3]

This disarray of the Christian community is an old sad story. One of the earliest scenes in the drama of church history shows us a demoralized church in Corinth, already ruptured by rival factions (I Cor. 1:10-13). St. Paul, from whom we hear the story, minces no words in his rebuke to these people. He makes it plain that he is not objecting to *diversity,* but to the fact that the factions in Corinth are hindering the church's mission to the unbelievers (I Cor. 3:1-23) and are separating the believers at the Table of the Lord (I Cor. 11:17-32).

Much later, the Christians in Ephesus are warned against disunity for the same reason: because it thwarts God's purpose "to gather all things together in a single whole, in Christ"[4] (cf. Eph. 1:10). Christians who have been

[3] Curtis B. Haley (ed.), "Fraternal Message to the General Conference of the Methodist Episcopal Church, South, April 29, 1938," *Journal of the Twenty-third General Conference of the Methodist Episcopal Church, South* (Nashville: Publishing House, Methodist Episcopal Church, South, n.d.), p. 358.

[4] Author's translation.

saved by the sheer mercy of God have only one appropriate response to make:

> . . . Speaking the truth in love, we are to grow up in every
> way into him who is the head, into Christ, from whom the
> whole body, joined and knit together by every joint with
> which it is supplied, when each part is working properly,
> makes bodily growth and upbuilds itself in love (Eph. 4:15-16).

But the clearest and most categorical affirmation, that
Christian unity is prerequisite to a fully effective Christian
mission, comes in our Lord's "High Priestly Prayer," in
John 17:20-23. Here Jesus prays for that unnumbered
multitude to whom the Gospel will be preached but who
will not hear it with believing hearts unless they see it
bodied forth in the Christian community.

> "I do not pray for these only, but also for those who are to
> believe in me through their word, that they may all be one;
> even as thou, Father, art in me, and I in thee, that they also
> may be in us, so that the world may believe that thou hast
> sent me. The glory which thou hast given me I have given
> to them, that they may be one even as we are one, I in them
> and thou in me, that they may become perfectly one, so that
> the world may know that thou hast sent me and hast loved
> them even as thou hast loved me."

The subsequent history of the church has been a sort of
commentary on the basic thesis of this prayer. When
Christians have been strong in their sense of community
with each other in Christ, they have usually been effective
in their mission to the world. Whenever they have fallen

into conflict and contradiction, the world has found it easy to ignore them or, even worse, to domesticate the churches as allies to rival secular interests.

It should be stressed, however, that the ideas concerning Christian unity expressed in the New Testament and by the early church do not confuse unity with uniformity. The New Testament writers make no bones about the tensions among the apostles, the diversities of their doctrines and polity, their rivalries—as between Peter and Paul (Gal. 2:11-14) or between Jerusalem and Antioch (Acts 15:5). The men who selected the books for the canonical New Testament took for granted the compatibility of real diversity with genuine unity. Thus, in the New Testament, we find a wide variety of teachings about the church and its corporate life called "Faith and Order" in the modern ecumenical movement. In this sense, the early church is still our model for true ecumenism for in it we see the various traditions of Petrine Christianity, and Pauline, Johannine, and Jacobite Christianity rooted in one basic faith and hope, united in baptism and in Holy Communion![5]

Diversity becomes divisive, however, when the differences between Christians tear at the essentials of faith and leave wounds to be infected by sectarian self-righteousness. When this happens, tensions turn into open conflict, dis-

[5] Cf. C. H. Dodd, *The Apostolic Preaching and Its Development* (New York: Harper & Bros., 1936) for a description of the similarities and differences between the various traditions represented in the New Testament: Petrine Christianity centering in Jerusalem until A.D. 70; the Pauline mission "to the Gentiles," with its base in Antioch; Johannine Christianity centered largely in Ephesus; Jacobite Christianity (Edessa) representing the further development of Jewish Christianity after the dispersion of the Jerusalem church. See also Jean Danielou, *The Theology of Jewish Christianity* (London: Darton, Longman and Todd, 1964).

agreements lead to overt repudiation. One of the most tragic instances of this came in the third and fourth centuries in "Africa," the Roman province which corresponded quite roughly to modern Tunis and Algeria. Carthage, its capital, was one of the most important centers of Christianity in the world and was, for a time, as strong as Rome. But then came the Donatist controversy and this unity and strength were shattered. The issue at stake did not concern fundamental Christian doctrine, but the thorny question of *ministerial ordination*. This was Christianity's first big fuss on this point but not the last, worse luck! What began as a religious conflict was further embittered by racial and political hatreds, and this, too, set an ugly precedent. The resulting turmoil so weakened both the church and the civil state that the whole region—and the Donatists, too —fell an easy prey to the marauding Vandals when they invaded Africa in 428-29 under Genseric. Three centuries later and nine hundred miles further east, the bitter rivalry between the "Monophysite" and "Orthodox" Christians (both professing the Nicene Creed and both claiming the episcopate in apostolic succession) so sapped the foundations of the Byzantine empire that in less than two generations the Moslem hoards had swept, virtually unopposed, across the Mediterranean seacoasts from Antioch to Gibraltar.

The story of Christianity's self-crippling is too long and far too complex to recount in any detail. But one more example, closer home, may be much more to the point. All of us are aware of the spirit of radical secularism in the modern world and of the fact that the Christian church exists in the world more by sufferance than with any profound authority. We know, too, that in many parts of the world toleration of the church has given way to repression or to outright persecution. What we may not realize is that one of the primal causes of this relegation of the churches to irrelevance goes back to the ghastly experiences in Europe during the sixteenth and seventeenth centuries, when "wars of religion" repeatedly devastated the lands and peoples and convinced many thoughtful men that Christianity—*divided* Christianity—was incorrigibly divisive and authoritarian. Slowly but surely even Christian statesmen came to prefer a fully secularized state over any state-church relationship they had ever known or could conceive. The notion of a free *and* united Christian community was beyond their imaginations, in view of their experiences with "holy wars."

Yet a blessing was gained from this havoc—it gave us our modern concepts of religious liberty and toleration. Men came to see that coercion in religion is finally self-defeating, that it is better to tolerate religious "error" than to kill or maim people in the interest of religious "truth." On the other hand, this disenchantment with religious strife also led to a wholesale rejection of the church's office and influence in political, economic, and social affairs. As a corollary to this there developed the notion that religion should be restricted to the domain of personal piety and private morality, a view still advocated by many Christians: let the churches "stick to religion" and leave the public affairs of mankind to secular control. As this new secularism spread and waxed confident, it began its bid to replace the church and to direct modern man's allegiance to new man-centered idolatries: communism, fascism, Nazism, nationalism, racism.

It is fashionable nowadays to bemoan the church's loss

of relevance and power and to account for this by one or another theory of the inadequacy of the church's methods and message. It is nearer the truth to say that modern man has found what for him are satisfactory substitutes for the church and her gospel, that he has come to doubt that Christians really mean what they say in their talk about "reconciliation" and "community" since they are manifestly unreconciled to each other when they mutually exclude each other from their holiest occasions (Baptism and the Lord's Supper). It is true that the traditional trappings of historical Christianity badly need updating. We Christians may welcome new versions of the gospel and new patterns of discipleship, but the world will still be deaf to *any* version of the Christian faith that does not prove itself in the love its believers manifest toward one another—that professes community and practices separation.

This is why it is valid to speak of the *scandal* of Christians in disunity—taking "scandal" in its root meaning in both Greek and English. For Greek-speaking Jews a *skandalon* was not a moral lapse to be mongered about by gossips—but rather some idea or act which, they thought, hindered belief or fostered disbelief (idolatry). This is its meaning in I Cor. 1:23. This is also its meaning according to the *Oxford English Dictionary* where the first definition of "scandal" is "something that hinders reception of faith . . . an occasion of unbelief . . ." The example there given, from Francis Bacon, is very apt for our whole argument: "Schisms are, of all others, the greatest scandals, because they corrupt or hinder faith."

The scandal of Christians in disunity does not consist so much in its effect upon Christians themselves as in its alienation of the world. The church's original warrant for existence was not that it might obtain special benefits for its own members but rather that it might carry out the Master's commission to "go into all the world, discipling all nations"[6] (Matt. 28:19). The unity of those ordained to this mission is both a directive and a function of the mission itself—"that the world may believe"!

The *scandal* of disunity, then, lies in its effect upon our witness to the world. Christianity has been a minority movement in the human community from the beginning. It is still a minority that is not even holding its own, comparatively speaking, with the staggering growth of the world's population and the rampant spread of secular humanism and atheism. It would be obviously false to attribute these developments solely to the disorders of the Christian community—but it is equally false to suppose that these disorders have had nothing to do with the decline of religion in the modern world. What else should we have expected of those to whom we preach "the unity of the Spirit in the bond of peace" when the bond of peace does not include a true mutuality of membership and ministry among all "bonded" Christians? Who is supposed to "discern the body [of Christ]" in the Lord's Supper when Christians are divided at the Lord's Table—when the Communion may be "holy" but plainly not communion?

At the Second World Conference of Faith and Order (Edinburgh, 1937) the chief Southern Baptist delegate, Dr. John R. Sampey, declined the invitation to participate in the Conference Communion Service because, as he said, it would be administered by a man not validly baptized. In this case the "unbaptized" man was William Temple,

6 Author's translation.

then Archbishop of York—and later of Canterbury—one of the ecumenical titans of this century. By the same token, however, Archbishop Temple would have refrained from the Communion in Dr. Sampey's church—or in a Methodist church—nor would Methodists have been welcome to the Lord's Table in an orthodox Lutheran congregation. We, who have grown up with these anomalies, take them for granted and have our answers ready for those who deplore them. But what is the unbeliever supposed to make of it—the African animist whose soul is being competed for by rival representatives of the one Body of Christ, or the American college student whose spiritual hunger is for authentic belonging to a truly universal community? I shall not soon forget the instance cited by a Uniate bishop in Rome, of two brothers (one Roman Catholic, the other Orthodox) being married in a Syrian town in the same house at the same time but in separate ceremonies conducted by their two respective pastors who refused to speak to each other. This was perplexing enough for the Christians, said the bishop, but the ones most deeply baffled—which is to say *scandalized* in the literal sense—were their Moslem neighbors.

There is a depressing abundance of evidence that denominational competition on "the mission fields" continues to project the image of Christianity as a congeries of rival groups as readily identified by their national origins as by their place in the Christian community. For example, there are five different Patriarchs of Antioch, none of whom lives in Antioch itself. Closer home, is there any serious doubt that the tangle of sectarian tensions in America (including the "sectarian atheists") has been one of the chief considerations influencing the Supreme Court in its series of decisions against the inclusion of the tokens of religious practice in public education?

There has been much talk of church renewal—and none of it needless. But renewal must show itself, first of all, in mission—for how can we convince men that God was in Christ reconciling *the world* to himself, when they can see that Christians are not reconciled to each other? How can Christians hope to unite mankind in peace and fellowship when they are still divided among themselves at their own baptismal fonts and communion tables? How can churches that will not risk any loss of their own institutional sovereignty persuade their members to risk more in the ventures of international cooperation? What can churches that look for all the world like avocational or recreational interest groups expect to achieve in the successive crises that are wracking our secular society in this age of rapid social change?

It would be absurd to claim that a united Christian community could solve all, or any, of these problems just by virtue of being united. But it would be an enormous gain if we could lessen the handicaps we have placed upon ourselves by "our unhappy divisions." At the very least, a united witness would make our Christian profession more credible to the world by lending reality to our proclamation of the glad tidings that God has reconciled us—and all mankind—to himself through pardoning and community-making, unifying love.

If we could agree that our interest in Christian unity comes from our concern for the effectiveness of the Christian mission, we could also be frank in our appraisals of the virtues and faults of the actual programs of ecumenical action that are being sponsored by our churches and by the various councils of churches—local, national, and worldwide. It is the devoted ecumenist—and not the sectarian—who should be the first to disavow all those starry-eyed enthusiasts who extol unity for the sake of unity. He should also reject those impatient prophets who refuse to reckon with the practical difficulties involved. It is the ecumenist who should disclaim the label of "indifferentism" by resisting the temptation to set aside all disputed points. He should refuse to conceal, water down, or even deny his own basic convictions in the interest of some spurious consensus that will not last. It is the veteran ecumenist—not the novice and certainly not the sectarian —who should resist the lure of "bigness" and the seductions of pomp and circumstance. It is an article of his creed that the basic unit of the universal Christian community is the local community of Christians—*all* the Christians in each place in valid communion with each other. The ecumenist knows, at least as well as any sectarian, that ecclesiastical power can corrupt as ruinously as any other power and he is, therefore, deeply averse to the fatal drift toward unchecked centralization of power and the bureaucracy and bureaucratic mentality it fosters.

The sincere ecumenist feels fully free to criticize the procedures of the ecumenical agencies created by the churches; he need not be overly defensive if others criticize these agencies for their failure to promote the ends specified by the churches themselves. None of these ecumenical agencies is a church—much less a "super-church"— nor do any of their officers and spokesmen acquire any other hierarchical authority than their own church membership. Their reports and statements have the legitimate character of items for study, reflection, and action in the churches. The reports, however, are badly misconstrued when regarded as *legislative acts,* as they have been called in the reckless, bitter attacks we have seen mounted against the National Council of Churches, the World Council of Churches, and occasionally, against the state and local councils. Such attacks are usually made by sectarians and reactionaries who recoil from the bare notion of Christians-in-true-community, and sometimes for reasons that are not really religious but political.

The mainspring of ecumenical concern in our time is the lively hope that has been raised in the hearts of Christian men—men of all sorts and conditions of churchmanship—that the unity of Christians will enhance the effectiveness of our proclamation of the gospel, that unity may be had without the loss of creative diversity, that we can move beyond our tragic history of internecine strife within the Christian family to a genuine reconciliation which would itself be a reconciling influence in the world. Each of us stands in one or another of the various Christian traditions. We rightly feel ourselves rooted in the life and agenda of a specific denomination and we would do well to take some pains to understand and to appropriate the vital treasures of our distinctive heritages and witness. No possible good will ever come from any simple-minded opposition of denominationalism versus ecumenism. We must beware, however, that our denominational loyalties do not serve us as excuses for continuing in the old ways under old triumphalist banners—or terrify us at the thought that a denominational death-and-resurrection may have to occur before we can be involved in the recovery of the wholeness of Christ's church.

Protestants have had a slogan that carries a profound

implication for our notions of Christian unity: *ecclesia semper reformanda*—"the church ought always to be in the process of being reformed." The least this can mean is that nothing in any church's institutional structures and processes is sacrosanct and exempt from reform and renovation. It can mean more: that every church is committed to a constant endeavor to express the *fullness* of Christian truth and experience, and is, therefore, open to responsible change and development toward that goal. But the *fullness* of Christian truth and the *wholeness* of the Christian community are coordinates: you cannot have the one without the other. Thus, rightly construed, *semper reformanda* is an ecumenical motto—and all the more so because its warrant is also that of all valid ecumenism.

Methodists have a peculiar history of being a church that has evolved from its origins as a religious society within another church (the Church of England). Many of the criticisms once levelled by Methodists against the Anglicans are now aimed at The Methodist Church, and some are pertinent. Moreover, many of our resistances to reform are remarkably similar to those which Mr. Wesley so strenuously deplored—*viz.*, our attachment to our particular *polity* (church order) as the essence of our distinctive mission in the world. By rights, however, we Methodists are committed to our patterns of *polity* only insofar as they really serve the Christian mission, "that the world may believe." It was not out of character, therefore, for a Methodist bishop to be the chairman of a section of the Oberlin Conference on Faith and Order, which hammered out a statement on ecumenical imperatives that might well speak for the rest of us:

". . . The faith we share is a common commitment to the high calling of God in Christ Jesus, and a common mission to bring to mankind the message of the great salvation he offers." It is this awareness of our unfinished task that relates the biblical imperatives to the contemporary scene, and gives them a relevance which might otherwise escape our attention. In our divided state we are not meeting the demands of our age; our ineffectiveness in mission compels us to heed more closely the biblical demands for unity. . . .

. . . Christ, who is ever present with his people, prays for our unity — a unity which must be manifest visibly and corporately to the world in order that men may believe the Gospel. Indeed, the unity of Christ's followers will be evidence to the world that God has sent his Son. The announcement that God was in Christ reconciling the world unto himself has an imperative corollary: he has entrusted to us the ministry of reconciliation. In fulfilling its mission, the church realizes its true unity and only through its unity may it fulfill its mission.

. . . Unity is not an option which we may take or leave; rather, if we are faithful to the Gospel which we have received and in which we stand, we must acknowledge that it is God's gift, God's demand, and God's promise. Christian faith means receiving this gift, obeying this demand, and hoping in this promise.[7]

The imperative to unity is the imperative to mission.

[7] Paul S. Minear (ed.), *The Nature of the Unity We Seek* [Official Report of the Oberlin Conference on Faith and Order, 1957] (St. Louis, Mo.: The Bethany Press, 1958), pp. 169-80.

CHAPTER TWO

CHRISTIANS
IN SEARCH OF
COMMUNITY

EVEN AFTER their violent schisms of the first half of the sixteenth century, neither the Catholics nor the Protestants could bring themselves to accept the fact of an irreparable loss of unity. The Catholics were determined to recover their lost provinces; the Protestants were determined to extend the Reformation over the whole of Europe. Both sides were bent on monopoly, for each in its own eyes was the sole authorized custodian of Christian truth—and, hence, of Christian community. Mortal combat and the "Wars of Religion" in France, the German Empire, and England left Europe in a shambles and in deep shock. By the end of the seventeenth century it was finally clear, even to the Christian partisans, that their lost unity could never be restored by force. It was a tragic lesson, learned at a frightful toll of blood and bitterness. It confirmed the secularists in their aversion to Christianity—so that Pierre Bayle could say of it that it was "a murthering and sanguinary religion,"[1] and a professed Christian like Pierre

---

[1] Peter Bayle, *The Historical and Critical Dictionary* (2d ed., London: Printed for J. J. and P. Knapton, D. Midwinter *et al*, 1736), III, 551, see under "Japan."

Charron could complain of the scandal of Christian disunity:

> In truth it is a strange thing, that the Christian Religion, which, being the only true one, as coming from God, ought to be indivisible, since there is but one God, and one Truth, should nevertheless be torn into so many Parts, and divided into so many contrary Opinions and Sects; insomuch that there is not any one Article of Faith, or Point of Doctrine, but what has been differently debated and contradicted by Sects and Heresies. . . . For it is a terrible thing to consider the Effects, which the Divisions of Christians have produced. In the first place, as to the Political State of the World, many Alterations and Subversions of Republics, Kingdoms, and Kingly Races, and Divisions of Empires, have happened, so far as to disturb the whole World with cruel, furious, and more than bloody Exploits, to the great Scandal, Shame and Reproach of Christendom: in which, under the Name of Zeal and Affection to Religion, each Party hates the other mortally, and thinks it lawful to commit all manner of hostilities.[2]

With considerable reluctance, Christians came to accept the notions of religious toleration and religious pluralism as the only viable alternatives to endless strife. Out of this came, naturally enough, the basic concept of "denominationalism," namely, that any group is entitled to a legal existence by whatever title it denominates itself, and is free to teach and practice its tenets unless they are plainly disruptive of public order. Thus, the whole complex pattern of religious toleration, of the separation of church and

2 Peter Bayle, *The Historical and Critical Dictionary* (2d ed.), II, 455, see under "Charron."

state, and the rampant confidence of the modern secular state in its omnicompetence, all stem from the scandal of Christians in disunity.

Forced to "tolerate" one another before the law, divided Christians accommodated themselves to a sort of ecclesiastical armistice. Denied the weapons of persecution, they fell back on verbal polemics. They could despise and denounce one another, but they had to keep the peace. Ink could be spilled recklessly, but not blood. Eventually, as the nineteenth century progressed, these conflicts began to lose their force and interest; estranged Christians began to develop a sort of etiquette and protocol for their conduct toward each other. It is this tradition of polite, even amicable, estrangement that most of us inherited and which we have adapted to the circumstances of our neighborhood and business life. Christians who cannot meet at the Table of the Lord may get along famously in the office, or in a bridge club, or on the golf course—by "keeping religion out of it."

Naturally enough, the varied denominations vied with each other in their evangelistic outreach and, increasingly, in the expanding field of foreign missions. The Protestants of the sixteenth-to-eighteenth centuries had been largely indifferent to missionary efforts outside Europe and North America. But it so happened that the development of denominational Protestantism coincided with and accompanied the colonial expansion of western Europe around the globe and brought about what Professor Latourette has called "the nineteenth, greatest of centuries" for the expansion of Christianity.

As the twentieth century dawned, signs began to multiply that denominational rivalry was approaching a point of diminishing returns. Religious pluralism was meeting its match in religious indifferentism. With the triumph of the scientific spirit and the expansion of secularism into the fields of education and human welfare, the Christian churches have been increasingly compelled to deal with the human problems of alcoholism, drug addiction, immorality, divorce, and juvenile delinquency which are the grim symptoms of the demoralization of modern society.

It would be quite wrong to suppose that Protestants have been indifferent to the problems of Christian unity. There is an excellent account of the episodic efforts of the Protestant pioneers of ecumenism—Jean du Bellay, Thomas Cranmer, Johann Amos Comenius, John Dury, and others—in Professor J. T. McNeill's remarkable survey, *Unitive Protestantism*. But Dr. McNeill also explains why, after their seed-sowing and reaffirmations of the ideal of Christian unity, their efforts bore so little fruit until the opening decade of the present century when three new factors converged to open a new chapter in the history of ecumenism.

The first of these was the missionary enterprise itself. Once the expansion of Christianity had reached round the world, rival missions and missionaries began to collide and compete in various sectors of "the heathen world" with resulting confusions that began to effect the basic character of the Christian mission. Professor W. Richey Hogg in his modern classic, *Ecumenical Foundations,* has told the dramatic story of how modern ecumenism emerged and found its vision and voice among those who had discovered, in the ends of the earth, that the world will not believe the Christian witness from churches in disarray.

A second prime source of ecumenical concern was the

Student Christian Movement in its various parts including, of course, the YM and YWCAs. Because of the experience of these organizations which functioned in the critical atmosphere of the modern college and university, a new breed of Christian youth began to make its presence felt in the Christian community. Having learned that disagreement and diversity need not cancel communication, the young men and women who belonged to these organizations were honestly perplexed by their discovery that there was often a more genuine community in the academic world than in the church. Some were disenchanted by this discovery and fell into J. S. Semler's facile separation between religious idealism (a good thing!) and theology (bad!). This dubious distinction has been resurrected in our time in the current vogue for "religionless Christianity," by which is meant something like "Christian devotion and social action without the institutional church and its inevitable corruptions."

Other students and student leaders, however, began to cast about for ways and means to recover the lost community that Christianity continued to profess. The first full generation of leadership in the modern ecumenical movement came from the alumni of these student movements. John R. Mott, one of the greatest leaders of them all, was executive director of the world YMCA before he became director of the International Missionary Council. It was for his services to the Student Christian Movement and the cause of missions that he was elected first honorary president of the World Council of Churches in 1948. Besides Mott, there was a host of others: William Temple, W. A. Visser 't Hooft, J. H. Oldham, Samuel M. Cavert, R. H. Edwin Espy. . . .

A third factor which helped to shift the spirit and temper of divided Christians was the appropriation by Christians of the methods and spirit of "Renaissance dialogue."

One of the significant sources of the new style in ecumenical theologizing has been our belated appropriation in this century of its roughly similar prototype in the European Renaissance of the 14th-16th centuries. It is now widely recognized that the men of the Renaissance developed the classical dialogue form into something distinctively new. From Petrarch through Bruni and Valla to Erasmus (and then on to Galilei and thereafter) one can trace the evolution of this new rhetorical mode. Its aim was persuasion, and it sought to achieve this by exhibiting ideas in collision but not in mortal combat. The author of a dialogue was expected to be able to state opposing positions fairly; else it could be retorted upon him that he had not understood them. The Renaissance dialogue did not hesitate to tip the scales in favour of one view above its competitors; but even the rejected views had to be assayed for their residues of truth.

. . . without this interpenetration of the Renaissance spirit of dialogue, it is hard to image how the old conventions of controversy could ever have been changed. Thus, in this sundered world of ours, living in deadly peril from the ruthless strife of ideologies, the pattern of dialogue has emerged to serve as an instrumentality of Providence in keeping the ecumenical movement from deadlock—or from flying apart![3]

The point to fix upon is that what has come to be called

3 Albert C. Outler, "From Disputation to Dialogue" [An address to The Fourth World Conference on Faith and Order, McGill University, Montreal, Canada, July 13, 1963], The Ecumenical Review, XVI, No. 1 (October, 1963), 15-17.

"the ecumenical movement" is actually a complex development of several combined concerns of Christian missionaries, educators, students, visionaries, and hard-headed ad-
ministrators, who became convinced of the new possibilities of Christian fellowship and cooperation in the new
situation facing Christianity in the modern world. Within
the span of a half century, a new era of church history has
opened up, a new frontier of Christian mission has been
crossed, basic changes in the climate of Christendom have
begun to take place—and the end is not yet, thank God.
We cannot, of course, tell that story here.[4] But we ought
to notice some of the landmarks on the way in order to
understand the basic issues and prospects in the current
situation.

The first and most important of all these ecumenical
landmarks was the memorable World Missionary Conference, held in Edinburgh, Scotland, June 14-23, 1910. This
marked the climax of earlier efforts at Christian cooperation in Europe, Asia, and America. Its delegates were
actually representatives of their respective missionary societies, and its leaders formed an elite corps of ecumenical
pioneers: J. H. Oldham (Scottish Presbyterian), Tissing-
ton Tatlow (Church of England), Archbishop Söderblom
(Lutheran), Robert E. Speer (Presbyterian USA), John
R. Mott (Methodist), and Bishop V. S. Azariah (Anglican, India).

The crucial importance of Edinburgh lies in the range
of ecumenical impulses that were generated there and that

---

[4] It has already been well told in W. Richey Hogg, *Ecumenical Foundations*
(New York: Harper & Bros., 1952); Ruth Rouse and Stephen Neill, *A History of the Ecumenical Movement* (Philadelphia: Westminster Press, 1954);
and Samuel McCrea Cavert, *On the Road to Christian Unity* (New York:
Harper & Bros., 1961).

have continued to develop in various directions ever since. The conference set up a Continuation Committee "to complete the work of investigation begun by the Conference, to carry out the suggestions made by the Commission reports, and, in council with the missionary societies, to work towards the formation of a permanent International Missionary Committee." This led eventually (in 1929, at Lake Mohonk, New York) to the formal organization of the International Missionary Council—the oldest and most effective of the agencies for ecumenical action in the first half of the century.

Edinburgh also reinforced the confidence of a small group of American Christians (Speer, Mott, Peter Ainslie, Shailer Mathews) who had already translated their notions of "practical Christian unity" into the Federal Council of the Churches of Christ in America (1908). The initial roster of this Council counted thirty denominations and its constitution declared its basic purpose: ". . . 'more fully to manifest the essential oneness of the Christian churches of America in Jesus Christ as their divine Lord and Savior [and] to express the fellowship and catholic unity of the Christian church.' "[5]

In Great Britain this concern for Christian cooperation in the area of Christian social ethics issued in a great Conference on Christian Politics, Economics and Citizenship (COPEC) at Birmingham, in April of 1924. On the Continent, the dynamic leadership of a great Lutheran, Archbishop Nathan Söderblom, primate of Sweden, opened the way for the first Universal Christian Conference on Life and Work which met in Stockholm in August of 1925. Incidentally, this conference marked the first

5 Samuel McCrea Cavert, On the Road to Christian Unity, p. 19.

time that Eastern Orthodox Christians had ever participated in such an interdenominational gathering, the first time that an assembly of western Christians had ever heard the Nicene Creed recited in the original—i.e., without the *filioque*—by the Greek Metropolitan Germanos.

The veterans of Edinburgh and Stockholm were wary of theological controversy. They agreed, however reluctantly, with Hermann Kapler's dictum (Hälsinborg, 1922): "Service unites; doctrines divide." But there were a few younger men, like Bishop Charles Henry Brent (an American Episcopalian who had been a missionary in the Philippines) who realized that Christian cooperation had a limited range unless it could be extended to a candid and probing dialogue on questions of "faith and order." Brent began his planning at Edinburgh in 1910, but it was not until 1927 (in Lausanne, Switzerland) that the first "World Conference on Faith and Order" was convened. It was a risky business and, even today, it seems a miracle that it did not founder on the jagged rocks of bigotry. Actually, it was an exciting revelation that there was more of a basic doctrinal consensus among the delegates than they had expected—and this they formulated into an important "Message to the Churches," which still is very much worth a careful reading.[6]

Two years later, on the Mount of Olives in Jerusalem, the International Missionary Council convened a great world conference vividly described by Dr. Hogg as "the first truly representative, global assembly of Christians in the long history of the church."[7] The influence of the

[6] See below, Appendix I, p. 117: *Lausanne's Message to the Churches.*

[7] W. Richey Hogg, *Ecumenical Foundations*, p. 244. It was indeed global, but not fully representative, for there were but a handful of the Orthodox and no Roman Catholics. The preceding year, Pope Pius IX had officially

Jerusalem Conference spread around the world and its
stirring Christ-centered "Message" made a profound im-
pression on even the conservatives who had been avowedly
suspicious of ecumenical missions. It, too, still has a vital
word for us today.[8]

The success of these experiments in Christian fellowship
gave increasing substance to the emerging vision of some
sort of world organization which would include all
churches willing to cooperate in Christian witness and
service and willing to seek, together, a more effective unity
in Word and Sacrament. At Oxford in July, 1937, a second Universal Christian Conference on Life and Work was
held and this was followed, in August, by the second World
Conference on Faith and Order in Edinburgh. The highlight of the second Edinburgh conference was a unani-
mously adopted statement on "the grace of our Lord Jesus
Christ"—a thorny theological issue that created great tension in the opening debates and might have disrupted the
conference. But when the final report was read to the
delegates, they responded with an unprecedented outburst
—the Doxology and an impromptu prayer of thanksgiving.[9]

The way toward an inclusive organization was now open
—and in the following May, in Utrecht, Holland, a Provisional Committee for the World Council of Churches in
Process of Formation was established and the first draft
of a constitution prepared for distribution to the churches
that had been participating in "Life and Work" and "Faith

forbidden Roman Catholic participation in such "pan-Christian assemblies." See below, Appendix II, p. 121: *Mortalium Animos*.

8 See below, Appendix III, p. 135: *The Message from Jerusalem*.

9 See below, Appendix IV, p. 141: *Edinburgh* (1937), "The Grace of Our
Lord Jesus Christ."

and Order" "for study and appropriate action." But in 1938 the world was drifting into a holocaust and a full decade passed before the World Council could come into formal existence. Yet, even during the ghastly decade from 1938 to 1948, the leaders of the Provisional Committee and of the International Missionary Council were able to bring off the most remarkable program of Christians in the service of peace in a world at war that has yet been chronicled.

When the World Council of Churches came into being in 1948 (in Amsterdam), the International Missionary Council preferred to continue as an independent agency— chiefly on the ground that the World Council of Churches was a council of *churches,* whereas the International Missionary Council had always been a council of *councils,* with a more flexible structure and working process. These two great ecumenical agencies, therefore, continued their work in effective cooperation but under separate management until the Third Assembly of the World Council of Churches at New Delhi in 1961 when the International Missionary Council merged with the World Council of Churches as one of its three major divisions. At New Delhi, the three pathways toward Christian unity that had been opened up at Edinburgh, fifty years before, finally converged.

It has always been denied officially, but the fact is that the institutional forms of the ecumenical movement from Edinburgh to New Delhi were largely shaped by the Protestants who predominated in their membership and management. Father Gustave Weigel used to speak of the World Council of Churches as "Protestantism, Incorporated." It is true that there were representatives of the Eastern Orthodox churches and of the so-called "lesser Eastern churches" (Armenian, Jacobite, Mar Thoma, and others) at all major conferences from Stockholm to New Delhi. But these representatives always came in small numbers and always with the express stipulation on their part that their participation in these conferences implied no willingness whatsoever to barter the eternal verities of Orthodox doctrine and holy tradition. This was made clear, conference after conference, by official statements approved by the Orthodox delegations. Of all these statements, the declaration made to the Oberlin Conference (1957), and entered in the Conference "minutes," is the most explicit—but not at all untypical:

> Christian love impels us to speak candidly of our conviction that the Orthodox Church has not lost the unity of the Church intended by Christ, for she represents the oneness which in Western Christendom has only been a potentiality. The Orthodox Church teaches that she has no need to search for a "lost unity," because . . . she *is* the *Una Sancta* and that all Christian groups outside the Orthodox Church can recover their unity only by entering into the bosom of that Church which preserved its identity with early Christianity. . . .
>
> The Orthodox Church . . . declares that she has maintained an unbroken continuity with the church of Pentecost by preserving the apostolic faith and polity unadulterated. She has kept the "faith once for all delivered unto the saints" free from the distortions of human innovations. Man-made doctrines have never found their way into the Orthodox Church.
>
> . . . We are bound in conscience to state explicitly what is logically inferred; that all other bodies have been directly or indirectly separated from the Orthodox Church. Unity

from the Orthodox standpoint means *a return of the separated bodies to the historical Orthodox, One Holy Catholic
and Apostolic Church.*[10]

This, incidentally, is actually more intransigent than the
Roman position and yet the Orthodox have been so gracious and brotherly about it that very few Protestants have
taken offense.

"Protestantism, Incorporated" or not, the World Council
of Churches has never thought of *restricting* the domain of
its ecumenical program to any separate segment of the
Christian community. Indeed, it has constantly sought to
widen its fellowship to include more and more churches
from both ends of the ecclesiological spectrum. The great
climax of this policy came at New Delhi with the entry of
the Orthodox churches of Rumania, Bulgaria, and Russia.
As a result, the Orthodox—in all of their exotic variety—
constitute a full third of the total membership of the World
Council of Churches. The same Assembly also welcomed
into membership the first applicants from the family of the
Pentecostals—two churches from Chile. (Ironically, some
of the tiny fraction of the votes opposing these admissions
came from the Orthodox delegations just previously
seated.) The Council, however, has made clear its eager-
ness to receive any and all of the disparate traditions of the
Christian community into its continuing quest for unity.

In spite of all this, there was always the gaping excep-
tion of the largest of all the Christian bodies: the Church
of Rome. During a full half century, the Church of Rome
had gone about its own self-contained business of evangel-

[10] Paul S. Minear (ed.), *The Nature of the Unity We Seek,* pp. 160-61.
[Italics added by author.]

ism and missions—and of outpopulating the Protestants. From 1921 through 1924 a small stir was created by a series of "conversations" between a small group of Roman Catholics, headed by Cardinal Mercier of Malines-Brussels (Belgium), and a matching team of Anglicans, headed by Viscount Halifax, at Malines. In 1928, however, Pope Pius XI firmly squelched all official Roman Catholic participation in any of these "pan-Christian" movements in his encyclical, *Mortalium Animos,* "On Fostering True Religious Unity." Here he warned against "religious indifferentism" and outlined the terms of "return to Rome," by which *true* unity could be had, by any and all, at any time.[11]

Despite this official line, informal and unofficial contacts between Catholic and Protestant ecumenists continued to develop. Roman Catholic scholars began the serious study of contemporary Protestant theologians. Protestants, interested in "corporate worship," began to explore the "liturgical revival" among Roman Catholics— discovering, to their surprise, that the great Catholic liturgists were striving for a simplification of Christian worship at its center, not for its ritual elaboration. The interest of Catholic scholars such as Canon Gustav Thils and Msgr. Thomas Sartory in the World Council of Churches mounted steadily throughout the decade of 1948-58. At Oberlin (1957) there were three Roman Catholic "observers," who participated actively in discussion groups; at New Delhi there were ten. Also at New Delhi, the Catholics provided some very much needed housing for the delegates to the Assembly. Thus, a curious situation was

[11]Of especial interest would be a comparative study of Appendix II, p. 121: *Mortalium Animos* and Appendix VIII, p. 175: the Vatican II's *Decree On Ecumenism* below.

developing—an active ecumenical dialogue between Romans and Protestants, despite Rome's official disapproval and the massive residues of Protestant suspicions of all Romans—and especially the genial ones!

When, therefore, Pope John XXIII (1959) announced his intention to convene a Second Vatican Council and included ecumenism on its agenda, nobody (Catholic or Protestant) knew quite what to expect, and nobody on either side would have dared predict what has actually come to pass. Along with the "normal" commissions to prepare for the Council, Pope John also established a Secretariat for Promoting Christian Unity, headed by two great scholars and statesmen: Augustin Cardinal Bea and Bishop Jan Willebrands. This Secretariat promptly established contact with the World Council of Churches and with the pan-denominational bodies of non-Roman Christians, inviting them to send official "delegated-observers" to the Council. These observers were received with unstinted hospitality, given access to all of the sessions and the documents of the Council, invited to debate the issues of the Council in weekly seminars with the bishops and theologians of the Secretariat, given the run of St. Peter's, received in private audiences by Pope John and later by Pope Paul. This was an unprecedented development in the history of such councils, and, when the history of Vatican II is written in due perspective, the contribution of the observers will be found to have been significant. By the same token, of course, the observers and their constituents learned more about the Roman Church through the Second Vatican Council than they had ever known before.

It must not be forgotten, however, that Vatican II was

chiefly a domestic affair of the Roman Catholic Church, an experiment in renewal and renovation [*aggiornamento*] concerned with basic transformations in Roman Catholic self-understanding as a church with respect to liturgy, polity, theology, missionary activity, education, social ethics, and other aspects. In terms of the quest for Christian unity, the outstanding achievements of Vatican II were its decrees *On Ecumenism, On Religious Liberty,* and *On the Catholic Attitude Toward Non-Christian Religions.* In the teeth of violent opposition (political *and* theological!) the Council denied the ancient canard that "what happened in [Christ's] passion could be charged against all the Jews then alive, and against the Jews of today." "The Jews," says the declaration *On the Habitude of the Church Toward the Non-Christian Religions,* "ought not ever to be presented as rejected or accursed as if this were a scriptural teaching . . . the church . . . decries hatred, persecution, displays of anti-Semitism, directed against Jews by anyone at any time."[12] The positive values in the non-Christian religions were also stressed as a basis for further dialogue and fellowship.

After a widely publicized controversy, the Council also passed and promulgated a declaration *On Religious Liberty* which puts the Catholic Church on record as acknowledging the sacred rights of conscience in matters of faith and worship—abandoning its old contention for the *ius gladii* ("the right of the sword" to coerce schismatics and heretics)—and basing itself on Christian confidence in the spiritual authority of Christian truth: "none to be forced to faith; none to be impeded in his search for truth."

---

[12] From Vatican II's declaration *On the Habitude of the Church Toward the Non-Christian Religions* (Rome: Typis Polyglottis Vaticanis, 1965).

In the decree *On Ecumenism* the Council gave the church a charter for ecumenical action in its dealings with "separated brethren." It begins (Chapter I) with a reminder to all Catholics that their only valid basis for ecumenism is in their own manifestations of Christian faith, love, and justice. It then spells out (Chapter II) the rules for the *practice* of ecumenism, allowing for prudent experiments in common prayer and social action. It takes a forward look towards the eventual goal of common worship in the sacraments (*communicatio in sacris*). It concludes (Chapter III) with a description—by Catholics for Catholics—of those valid elements of Christian faith and order in the non-Roman churches—Orthodox, Anglican, and Protestant—that should be recognized by Catholics. And it must be said that these delineations of non-Roman churches are more generous and gracious than anything which has been produced thus far by a non-Roman church to describe the Romans![13]

What this whole story adds up to is that in our own lifetime, a major transformation has begun, affecting every part of Christendom. In a half century, we have moved from mutual toleration to mutual recognition, from disputation to dialogue. We have discovered the present fact of our God-given unity in Christ, and we have come to dream of the possible realization of the fullness of this unity, despite our uneasy awareness that its coming will drastically alter some of our cherished conventions.

A new spirit is abroad in the Christian community—a new hope, a new imperative. As Pope Paul VI said to the Observers (September 29, 1964): "An abyss of diffidence and skepticism has been mostly bridged over . . . a new

[13]See below, Appendix VIII, p. 175: Vatican II's *Decree on Ecumenism.*

method has been affirmed, a friendship has been born, a hope has been enkindled, a movement is underway, praise be to God who, we sincerely believe, 'has also given his Holy Spirit to us' " (I Thess. 4:8).

At the heart of this new spirit is the disposition to learn from other Christian traditions and to expose our own to the examination of others, knowing that these experiences will work unpredictable changes in us all. The new hope that has sprung up is that Christian unity may be more than a pious aspiration and that we may move toward this distant goal without haste or hesitation. The new imperative is that we venture out of our denominational citadels to seek out our separated Christian brethren and, with them, find new force and effectiveness in our own Christian witness and service in the world.

Who will deny that it is the Holy Spirit of God who has set us on this pathway and who is our Paraclete, our Counsellor and Guide, for the journey? Only the naive will imagine that the way is short or easy. Only the bigots will suppose that it will end at the place *they* never left. But even the beginning of the journey has generated a new sense of our *koinonia,* our "fellowship" in Christ, and new expectations of renewal and effective mission. Such an experience has become, for a rapidly increasing company, a veritable means of grace.

CHAPTER THREE

THE NATURE
OF THE UNITY
THAT WE SEEK

WE HAVE now said, in different ways and in various contexts, that the essential thesis of the ecumenical movement is that unity is in order to mission; that Christians are committed to the quest for unity to the end that the fullness of the church may be manifested in the world, in witness and service: "that at the name of Jesus every knee should bow—in heaven, on earth, and in the depths—and every tongue confess, 'Jesus Christ is Lord,' to the glory of God the Father" (Phil. 2:10-11, NEB).

But this declaration leaves somewhat vague the sort of unity that would best achieve this end, or that would best serve the Christian mission; nor have we estimated the nature of the changes that may come in the course of further developments in the ecumenical enterprise. There are more people who are kindly disposed toward unity as an idea than there are those who are clear as to what it means or what it will cost. Thus there are those who are ready to join the ecumenical dialogue but who become fearful or obdurate when "dialogue" passes over into actual negotiation. And there are also those who consider themselves as special guardians of their own traditions, commissioned to see to it that no notion of unity is allowed that might involve significant loss or change, no matter what the gains might be. On the other extreme, there are the ecumenical zealots who are ready for union *now,* who reject all hesitations about full communion, who are impatient with the laggard pace of progress toward the ecumenical goal. The footdraggers are fearful of the future; the zealots scornful of the past. In between them, the majority of the folk in the churches would seem to be governed by the law of inertia and "remain at rest or in uniform motion in a straight line unless acted upon by some external force."

This problem of the nature of the unity with which we are, or ought to be, concerned has baffled ecumenists all along. In the beginning, it was rather carefully avoided for the obvious reason that the Orthodox and the hitherto conventional Roman answers—"Return to us from whom you strayed"—were unthinkable to Protestants, and also for the less obvious reason that the basic connotation of Christian unity to most people was, and still is—*merger!* Moreover, since *merger* has always had, for most people, the unhappy connotation of "swallowing" or "being swallowed up," it carried with it an implicit indignity, especially to those who suspected that it might be *their* destiny to be swallowed up! A further complication in the problem of determining a valid and feasible concept of unity is the fact that most of us begin with our own church as our unconscious model for the united church—and this makes for ambiguities in our appraisals of the other churches involved. As Professor Watson has put it:

We cannot all think alike, and therefore we cannot all worship alike. There are bound to be diverse expressions of the

Christian faith and life. What is more, each of us is bound to think his own denomination the best there is; otherwise, we would presumably not belong to it. But there is a difference between believing your own to be the best and believing it to be the only right one.[1]

But what happens when Christians from several different denominations—each believing their own the best though not the only right one—attempt to formulate even a tentative definition of unity? Logically, it would be a matter of several "bests" (a contradiction in terms) trying to agree on a relative approximation to "the only right one" —and this is the very nub of the confusion in the ecumenical enterprise.

One of the traditional ways of transcending this deadlock of plural absolutes has been to strike for agreement on the *essentials* of Christian doctrine and polity and agree to differ on *non-essentials*. This is the plea of Meldenius' famous aphorism: "Unity in essentials, liberty in non-essentials and charity in both." But the obvious question leaps at you: who is to decide where the line falls between the two, and by what norm will it be drawn? All the different "confessions" of the various churches that have them (and, incidentally, the Methodists never have had one of their own!) profess to set forth only "the essentials." And when they disagree, as they do, what then?

In the early age of modern ecumenism, there were new experiments in the reformulation of the Christian essentials, in summary form, as the basis for unity among those

[1] Philip S. Watson, *The Message of the Wesleys* (New York: The Macmillan Co., 1964), pp. 58-59.

who would agree that these were, in fact, adequate summaries. Nothing essential was to be omitted, nothing nonessential insisted upon. The most widely discussed of these ecumenical summaries was set forth in 1846 by The Evangelical Alliance:

"(1) The Divine inspiration, authority, and sufficiency of the Holy Scriptures; (2) The right and duty of private judgment in the interpretation of the Holy Scriptures. (3) The Unity of the Godhead, and the Trinity of Persons therein. (4) The utter depravity of human nature in consequence of the fall. (5) The incarnation of the Son of God, his work of atonement for sinners of mankind, and his mediatorial intercession and reign. (6) The justification of the sinner by faith alone. (7) The work of the Holy Spirit in the conversion and sanctification of the sinner. (8) The immortality of the soul, the resurrection of the body, the judgment of the world by our Lord Jesus Christ, with the eternal blessedness of the righteous, and the eternal punishment of the wicked. (9) The Divine Institution of the Christian Ministry, and the obligation and perpetuity of the ordinances of Baptism and the Lord's Supper."[2]

A far more compact—and more controversial—minimum statement of Christian essentials was proposed by the Anglicans, first by the American Episcopalians at Chicago in 1886 and then by the bishops of the Lambeth Conference of 1888. This is now widely known as "The Lambeth Quadrilateral":

We believe that the visible unity of the Church will be found to involve the wholehearted acceptance of:

[2] William Adams Brown, *Toward a United Church* (New York: Chas. Scribner's Sons, 1946), p. 27.

A. The Holy Scriptures of the Old and New Testaments, as 'containing all things necessary to salvation,' and as being the rule and ultimate standard of faith.

B. The Apostles' Creed, as the Baptismal Symbol; and the Nicene Creed, as the sufficient statement of the Christian faith.

C. The two Sacraments ordained by Christ Himself — Baptism and the Supper of the Lord — ministered with unfailing use of Christ's Words of Institution, and of the elements ordained by Him.

D. The Historic Episcopate, locally adapted in the methods of its administration to the varying needs of the nations and peoples called of God into the Unity of His Church.[3]

The difficulty here, and in all such distillations, is that dissent on one point nullifies agreement on the others. For example, the Methodists are committed by their own traditions to *A, B,* and *C*—but they boggle at *D* as non-*essential.* Other Protestants find that *A* is far too vague or that *B* implies an unacceptable distinction between the Scriptures as "the *standard* of faith" and the Nicene Creed as "the *statement* of the Christian faith."

And so it goes—not only with this but every such summation of *all* the essentials and nothing but the *essentials.* Moreover, even where such summaries are accepted, it is then often discovered that the question of "liberty" in some of the *non*-essentials is not as easily handled as one might think. We are familiar with what Professor C. H. Dodd used to call "our unavowed motives" for intransigence: our inherited loyalties and biases that cannot honestly be defended as *essential,* but which we shrink from having

[3] F. L. Cross (ed.), *Oxford Dictionary of the Christian Church* (London: Oxford University Press, 1957), p. 781.

labeled *non*-essential. It begins to be evident that unity cannot be achieved through creed-making, for it is only Christians-already-in-unity who can make a creed that commands consensus, not the other way around.

The recognition of all these pitfalls in the way toward unity "in the essentials" has led a great many Christians in our time to rest their "ecumenical" hopes on Meldenius' *third* phrase "charity (*caritas*) in both [essentials and non-essentials]"—and to think of Christian unity in terms of spiritual union and Christian fellowship which springs from the love that Christians owe one another anyway. This is unity at a level that does not grapple with the nettles of theology and does not demand much by way of institutional change. It is a sort of *ecumenism within the status quo*—and it has the merit of being minimally acceptable to all but the outright bigots. "Unity in the Spirit" is at least the foundation of all ecumenism.

It must be true for most of us that our interest in Christian unity was first generated by one or another profound experience of spiritual fellowship with other Christians whom we had not known before and whose richness and vitality in faith and worship was a revelation to us. What happened in most of these encounters was that our prejudices began to dissolve as we found ourselves in a new atmosphere—an atmosphere which generated understanding of others and of ourselves and revealed new treasures of the Spirit in unsuspected places. As at Pentecost, the "strangers" heard and understood the Galileans— so in genuine spiritual fellowship, *koinonia,* we "Galileans" will discover that we too can hear and understand the "strangers." Many of our most cherished memories are those of interdenominational services in which, at some point or other, we knew in our hearts, more deeply than ever before, that we were already one in a God-given unity in Christ that crosses all the barriers of creed and polity, of rite and ceremony, of race and caste and culture.

My Methodist forebears taught me (among other more affirmative things) that Episcopalians tend to be both snobbish and ritualistic, and it was never clear to me which of these was the greater fault. My own ecumenical encounters with Episcopalians have happily unsettled that self-righteous stereotype. My Protestant forebears also taught me that the Roman Catholic Church was "the synagogue of Satan" and that Roman Catholics are out to take over, by fair means or foul. My experiences in Rome and with Catholics in America have taught me to be ashamed of this libel. Our dreams of a unity yet to be achieved must be grounded in the reality of the unity that we already have in foretaste, the unity first realized in our affirmations of spiritual unity with our separated brethren. The scandal of our divisions has been mitigated, at least for us, by the joyful recognition of this present spiritual unity of heart and hope.

So far, so good. But here is also the point of temptation: to settle for this "unity in the Spirit" as the limit of our ecumenical aspirations. The lure of this limit is strong for two reasons—one positive, the other negative. Positively, "spiritual fellowship" is a giant step beyond the old patterns of hedgehog independence which we can no longer sincerely defend. It means the end of the old order of spiritual isolation. Negatively, however, the modes of spiritual fellowship thus far developed leave the old order of visible divisions open and glaringly revealed before the eyes of the world. Spiritual unity brings excitement and joy to the Christians involved, but it does little to overcome their estrangements in matters of polity, the ministry, and the sacraments. The world, to which we are sent as witnesses of the gospel of God, will scarcely be bowled over by our intramural festivities which leave us still divided in our pulpits, at our fonts, and at the Table of the Lord. There is something false and unreal about a *spiritual* fellowship that cannot evolve into something tangible—that gives us an emotional lift and then leaves us undisturbed in our old ways and loyalties.

It seems evident, therefore, that in order for real Christian community to exist spiritually among the churches, more unity in the structural, tangible area of the church's life must be achieved. Christian unity on the spiritual level is prevented by disunity on the concrete visible level. . . . it is in two main areas that this present concrete disunity reveals itself: in the area of polity and sacramental practice and in the area of theology or faith. Here what is lacking is on the one hand a unified pattern of ministry or of orders, of organizational structure, and on the other hand a unity of confession or of theology.[4]

It would seem inevitable, therefore, that every church in Christendom must, with greater or less reluctance, look ahead toward developments that will carry them beyond this first stage of spiritual ecumenism—directly toward true unity in the *Holy Spirit*. For it is the office of the Holy Spirit to build (edify) the church and all believers in truth and power and *koinonia*. It is the Spirit who vali-

---

[4] Langdon B. Gilkey, "The Unity of Spirit and the Forms of Church Unity," *Christian Unity in North America*, ed. J. Robert Nelson (St. Louis, Mo.: The Bethany Press, 1958), p. 120.

dates the church's ministry, her sacraments, her mission!

But churchmen are inherently conservative, and many who have been willing to venture beyond the easy joys of spiritual unity are still looking for a way to avoid going much further. They would, therefore, be happy to alight at the halfway house of "federal union." This notion has appeared in several different guises—all of which amount to the inclusion of the separate churches, *just as they are,* in a still wider organization that would unite the membership of the churches but not their clerical orders; that would foster various cooperative programs of Christian service and social action at home and broad; and that would consolidate as many as possible of the overlapping administrative processes in the churches. In short, it would be federal union if the members of the National Council of Churches or the World Council of Churches were to reconstitute the Council as a church in its own right— with the member-churches retaining their respective autonomies in *non*-essentials *and* in the matter of the ministry and the sacraments.

It is common knowledge by now that there are many areas of human need where the churches can render marvelous service when they unite on the platform of their mutual concerns for the dignity of the human person, for elemental justice and public morality, for peace and brotherhood. Where our humanity is at stake, or the rightful needs of our neighbor, our guidelines are given in the Great Commandment (Matt. 22:39; Mark 12:31; Luke 10:27) and they need not be blurred by the thorny problems of doctrine and polity. Nothing can justify a Christian standing aloof from his fellow Christians who have set their hands and hearts to a mission of service in loving solidarity with other human beings in their pains and hungers and desolations. Moreover, it is a tragic misunderstanding of the true nature of the Body of Christ for Christian denominations to attempt to go it alone in their involvements in these universal human causes or to seek denominational credit for what they may do in some cooperative venture.

Yet, while these patterns of "Christian cooperation" and "federal union" are valid, they are not sufficient. For *every* effort in Christian service—"faith working through love" (Gal. 5:6)—is rooted in the saving work of God in Christ and in the life of worship that celebrates this gospel of grace. Thus, even a working consensus in practical Christian service will lead, eventually, to the doctrinal questions of the nature of the church and of the sacramental character of Christian love-in-action. And this brings us to the anomaly of Christians who can work and suffer together in the service of God's kingdom, yet cannot gather together around the Lord's Table. One reaction—all too easy—is to let this difficulty relegate the sacraments to the margin of Christian concern. But this is the way that can lead to the relegation of the church itself to the same marginal position. For one's beliefs about the church and the sacraments are integral and they vary in direct proportion to each other. And, once the Christian passion for human welfare—however devoted and "prophetic" it may be in the beginning—is dissociated from the community of Christians gathered about the Cross of Christ (*viz.,* the Lord's Table), the consequence is inevitable. It is the radical secularization of human concern—the relinquishment of the social, civil, and moral responsibility of the church to the state—and we know what that sad end will bring from the depressing history of "social reform." For secular moralism is even *more* prone to hypocrisy and self-righteousness than is the moralism of those Christians who fail to match their witness with their works. The civil rights revolution was (and still is) an eminently just cause in which a *united* Christian community could have *led the way* so that American society would not now have to reckon with the ambivalent residues of so many remaining conflicts.

We have seen that, at the beginning of the century, there was almost no realistic hope of "organic union," that such reunion was generally taken to mean "return" or "merger" and, on either ground, was deemed undesirable. We have also seen how the notions of "spiritual ecumenism" and "federal union" have greatly served the cause of unity—but with manifest limitations that are increasingly felt as their good essences are realized. Thus, slowly but with a massive logic, the conviction has grown that the eventual goal of Christian ecumenism has to be the full, free communion of all Christians, not only in "the unity of the Spirit" and in all forms of courtesy, reciprocity, and co-operation, but also in a universal community of membership and ministry.

The crucial problem in trying to envisage any such community is, of course, focused on the paradox of the opposing poles of unity *and* freedom that must be maintained in any vital concept of *organic* union. In the course of Christian history these poles have tended to drift apart. In times of great external pressure on the church, there has been a tendency to stress the defensive values of *unity* with a corresponding de-emphasis on freedom. In times of reformation and revolution the passion for freedom has tended to sacrifice continuity and unity. In all times and in each case the New Testament is regularly cited as a warrant for whatever is being done. The New Testament ideal is plainly that of unity-in-diversity (or freedom-within-a-disciplined-community) but the Catholics tend to stress *"the unity* of the Spirit in the bond of peace," while the Protestants are appealing to Galatians 5:1 as their charter for freedom in Christ, and the sectarians are citing still another Pauline text, "Therefore come out from them, and be separate from them, says the Lord, and touch nothing unclean" (II Cor. 6:17—cf. Isaiah 52:11). The Catholic traditions stress *unity*—without rejecting the prime significance of diversity—but they manifest their diversity chiefly through the extraordinary proliferation of their "religious orders." There are more monastic orders, societies, and institutes in the Roman Catholic Church than there are Protestant denominations—and these various orders exhibit a startling (to us!) spectrum of different "rules" and patterns of communal life.

Protestants, on the other hand, have emphasized the higher value of Christian *freedom,* even while they regularly profess their deep concern for Christian *unity.* What usually happens, however, is that unity is conceived of in eschatological terms—which is a fancy way of saying that unity is an ideal existing "in heaven" or in "the church invisible" or that it is "a spiritual reality"—real to the eyes of faith despite the tragic appearances of estrangement in the church visible. There is a tinge of irony here but also a profound truth. There *is* such a thing as "our God-given unity in Christ" of which the ecumenical reports speak so glibly—a unity we can perceive by faith but have not yet achieved in fact. In a very real sense, the unity we seek is a realization of the unity that we already have—*eschato-logically*.[5] Meanwhile the integrity of faith depends on the *freedom* of faith: man before God, man responsible to God, the Christian man in freedom and travail, "above all earthly powers." Any fruitful vision of Christian community must take seriously this paradox of the Catholic concern for unity and the Protestant principle of man's freedom under God.

We must face the further fact that we cannot construct an image of the unity we seek out of the respective self-images of the divided churches, as they presently understand themselves and their relations with other churches. One of the great triumphs of the ecumenical dialogue has been to bring us to the point where all confess that, in *some* sense or other, all the trinitarian churches are "equal"—but we are also still at the stage where some of the churches insist, in good conscience, that they are more equal than others!

This situation has, naturally enough, hounded the World Council of Churches from the beginning. In 1950, its Central Committee issued what has come to be known as "The Toronto Statement"—an attempted explanation of the relations between "the Church, the churches and the World Council of Churches." One of its chief practical aims was to assure prospective applicants for membership that "no church need fear that by entering the World Council of Churches it is in danger of denying its own heritage." To this end the statement began with a quite proper and flat denial that the World Council of Churches is "a super-church" or "the world church" or "the holy

[5] Cf. Albert C. Outler, "The Church Unity We Have," *Christian Unity in North America*, ed. J. Robert Nelson (St. Louis, Mo.: The Bethany Press, 1958).

Catholic church" spoken of in the creeds. It then went on to affirm that the World Council of Churches, like all other ecumenical agencies, is an instrumentality of the churches to serve them in bringing them together in meaningful ways "for the study and discussion of the issues of church unity." No further effort was made to specify the kind of unity to be studied and discussed. But the nerve of the whole statement was the passage which amounted to a rather tense compromise between the Orthodox claim to be the *Una Sancta* (the one holy church), and the Protestant refusal to accept *the negative implications* of that claim: "The member churches of the World Council consider the relationship of other churches to the Holy Catholic Church which the Creeds profess as a subject for mutual consideration. *Nevertheless, membership does not imply that each Church must regard the other member Churches as Churches in the true and full sense of the word.*"[6]

This impasse was a clear warning that further ecumenical progress depended on a breakthrough at this particular point. Thenceforth this theme, "the nature of the unity we seek," came to be a logical focus for ecumenical analysis and experimentation.[7] The Oberlin Conference (1957) came up with a statement that marked a decisive step beyond Toronto:

. . . the Church is God's Church and [its] unity is his unity. This unity, we believe, is to be:

— A unity in Christ who died for us, is risen, regnant, and

6 See below, Appendix V, p. 147: *The Toronto Statement.*

7 Cf. the author's "experiment" with it in *The Christian Tradition and the Unity We Seek* (New York: Oxford University Press, 1957).

will come again to gather together all things in his judgment and grace;

— A unity in adoration of God — one offering of wonder, love and praise;

— A unity of declared faith, sounding the vast Amen of the whole Church's believing life through all the centuries;

— A unity of bearing one another's burdens and sharing one another's joys;

— A unity in which every ministry is a ministry of and for all the members, bound together in a worshipping and sacramental community;

— A unity in mission to the world, originating with, sustained by and offered to the one Christ, and conducted with such transparency of love and faithfulness that the world will believe in him;

— A unity possessing rich variety in worship, life and organization.[8]

The core of this description of unity was the sentence about the mutuality of ministry and membership, "bound together in a worshipping and sacramental community." For this is precisely what the Orthodox, Romans, and Anglicans—and Lutherans on other grounds—have not been prepared to concede on any terms other than some formula of "re-ordination" which, to the rest of us, means repudiation of even the good things in our traditions.

At a meeting of the Working Committee of Faith and Order (in Spittal, Austria, 1959) Bishop Lesslie Newbigin and I were assigned the task of producing a draft of a possible description of "the unity we seek" that might be presented to the forthcoming meeting of the Commission

[8] Paul S. Minear (ed.), *The Nature of the Unity We Seek*, p. 29.

on Faith and Order at St. Andrew's in 1960. The fourth or fifth version of our text was approved, provisionally; no first draft of anything has ever been accepted in any ecumenical gathering, and this is emphatically as it should be. It was then presented at the St. Andrew's meeting and adopted, with minor amendments. The following year, at New Delhi, the "St. Andrew's Statement" was again slightly amended and used as the basis of the World Council Assembly's statement on unity:

> We believe that the unity which is both God's will and his gift to his Church is being made visible as all in each place who are baptized into Jesus Christ and confess him as Lord and Savior are brought by the Holy Spirit into one fully committed fellowship, holding the one apostolic faith, preaching the one Gospel, breaking the one bread, joining in common prayer, and having a corporate life reaching out in witness and service to all and who at the same time are united with the whole Christian fellowship in all places and all ages in such wise that ministry and members are accepted by all, and that all can act and speak together as occasion requires for the tasks to which God calls his people.[9]

Perhaps the most important thing about *this* "description" is its measure of the progress in the discussion beyond the impasse at Toronto. It was, moreover, an earnest endeavor to deal fairly with *both* the poles of unity *and* freedom—and the Orthodox did not veto it.[10]

---

9 See below, Appendix VII, p. 165: *The New Delhi Report.*

10 Also see footnote No. 1 on p. 126 in *The New Delhi Report* (New York: Association Press, 1962). This refers to a statement prepared by the Orthodox delegations expressing their usual reservations about the "Re-

It cannot be claimed that this New Delhi statement was a breakthrough to anything close to a working formula for actual church unity negotiations. But it does provide an honest inventory of the main items that must be listed on any future agenda of such negotiations and it does highlight the "target issue" in the whole complex problem: "the whole Christian fellowship . . . whose *ministry and members are accepted by all.*" This was further commented on by the Section on Unity:

> All agree that the whole Body is a royal priesthood. Yet one of the most serious barriers to unity is our diverse understanding of the nature of the ministry within the corporate priesthood. . . . There are those, for example, who affirm the necessity of an episcopally ordained ministry in the apostolic succession while others deny that it is essential for the true Church. . . .[11]

If most of this sounds rather trite now, it is because we have had long enough to live with it to let its main notions seep into our ecumenical consciousness. For this is the way progress is made: a loggerhead-issue is described as clearly and candidly as possible, with no premature answers supplied. Then, in the ensuing reflections of the various parties, slight shifts in perspective tend gradually to move the whole discussion forward, toward the point where another forward step is possible.

The growing conviction that we cannot set our ultimate goal at less than organic union—however many proximate

port of the Section on Unity" as a whole. They did not, however, insist on its being printed in the Report itself.

[11]See below, Appendix VII, p. 165: *The New Delhi Report.*

goals we may have to settle for *ad interim*—has been matched by the dawning realization that we may be nearing the point where we can think, vaguely to be sure, of a united Christian community really united in *communicatio in sacris* (in membership, ministry, and sacraments) in which the distinctive witness of divers denominations, functioning as "orders," "societies," or "movements" under their own self-appointed heads, will be conserved within a wider catholic perimeter, organized constitutionally on some collegial and conciliar pattern. If *this* becomes the shape of the future, we might have a real alternative to the paralyzing fear that Christian unity portends some sort of totalitarianism. As more and more Christians come to see the bare possibility that Christian unity and Christian liberty can, and ought to, be coordinated, then their hopes and hungers will hasten the day when God will show us the way to its actual achievement.

The Orthodox still stand by their conviction that they constitute the only true and immaculate Christian tradition—and we must continue to respect them for their fidelity to this self-understanding. They are, typically, very gracious and gentle in their expositions of their views and very patient with the rest of us in our laggard reactions. But for the overwhelming majority of Protestants, this formula for unity is both incredible and unacceptable—if only for the fact that even if Orthodoxy's guardianship of the apostolic tradition has been faithful and valid, *relatively speaking,* its present claim to being or becoming the universal ecclesial institution is plainly untenable and its relationship to modern society and culture is patently archaic. For the Christian community to return to where the Orthodox now stand would be a *regression* into an alien past for which there is no justification—biblical, historical, or ecclesiological. The time has come when this must be said to them in as gracious and candid a manner as they have shown toward us.

Before the Second Vatican Council, one would have had to say something similar about the Roman Catholic prescription for Christian unity—with the added comment that the Roman Church had been markedly less gracious and patient with us than had the Orthodox. Now, however, the situation has changed so radically that one hardly knows what their new "terms of unity" may amount to. When the Council began, one heard frequent references to "the return of the separated brethren to Mother Church" who was now disposed to make their homecoming as painless as possible. But long before the Council's adjournment, this sort of language had been replaced almost entirely by such phrases as "the recomposition of unity," "the reconstituted unity of the People of God," and others. Indeed, the most significant practical aspect of the decree *On Ecumenism* is that it interprets unity as a cause with an open future, a goal toward which all parties may move expecting further changes that are now unforeseeable.

Surely the only conceivable approach to unity is forward, toward some convergence, in God's good time, of the straggling bands of the pilgrim People of God in their uneven progress toward "the Promised Land." The only unity worth seeking is that in a community of faith and grace and freedom, truly catholic and vitally evangelical, rooted in the Christian past but dynamically responsive to the opening frontiers of the modern world. The unity we seek is in the community of *all* the Creator's children who are one in Christ in the unity of the Holy Spirit, and thus truly members one of another. We can, as yet, envisage this unity only "through a glass darkly." But we have had a foretaste of it in our ecumenical experiences and we have recognized that its only source is God's grace in Christ Jesus our Lord. Such unity will come, if ever, less from our zeal and diplomacy than from our deepened understanding of God's grace, our renewed wills to do his service, and our awakened love of all God's children for whom Christ died. When we are really ready to offer our "distinctive" traditions and treasures as gifts to the whole family of God, willing for them to be refined and transmuted, even "so as by fire" (I Cor. 3:15), then we will be ready for God's gift of renewal, manifesting itself not only in our corporate union but also and eminently in our united mission—"that the world may believe!"

CHAPTER FOUR

METHODISM IN
THE ECUMENICAL
MOVEMENT

As WE have seen, the modern ecumenical movement is remarkably composite in its character. Each of the main traditions in the Christian community has had a shaping influence on the movement as a whole and each, in turn, has been affected by its participation in the ecumenical experience. No single church or church family has claimed or had a monopoly in the movement; none has tried to dominate it. All have brought with them their various inheritances to share and mingle with the others.

By the same token, however, this experience of mutual sharing makes it all the more imperative that we, as Christians in our separate traditions, understand ourselves and our heritage more fully and critically in order to share more effectively in the ongoing dialogue. Every denomination has acquired, in its own cherished folklore, a cluster of myths and stereotypes which serve as rallying points for self-righteous memories of the past, reverberators of bygone tensions and triumphs. We know, for example, how the Roman Catholics have insisted on papal primacy more than on some of their other cardinal concerns because, at least in part, this was the focal point of the Protestant attack against them. Again, Anglicans have italicized their claim to "the historic episcopate *in apostolic succession*" because Rome has rejected it and the Protestants have denied that it constitutes an "essential." Lutherans have laid great stress upon their possession of "pure doctrine." Calvinists, until recently, have seemed predestined to make of predestination a battle cry. Baptists and Disciples have long been zealots for their distinctive witness to "believer's baptism" (by immersion) and congregational polity. The Orthodox are still confident that they, alone, have preserved *the* Holy Tradition, to which the Romans reply that this is scarcely the case since they have been out of communion with the See of Peter for nine centuries. And so it goes. In each case what is called "our distinctive witness" seems to consist, at least in part, of the scar tissue formed over the ruptures that set us on our separate ways as denominations.

All our cherished "distinctive" emphases are interesting and important. They must be understood if there is ever to be any real comprehension of the ecumenical situation. But they are also awkward because, in actual practice, they complicate the dialogue with the emotions aroused by twinges from old hurts. These feelings are so much a part of our self-understandings that we tend to insist upon their recognition by others as preconditions for serious negotiation—and that usually lands us in deadlock. How *are* the Orthodox and the Roman Catholics and the Anglicans ever to settle their mutually exclusive claims with respect to the episcopate? How *are* episcopal and non-episcopal churches ever to unite their ministries without unworthy compromise? How *are* church polities as different as the Methodist and the Baptist ever to be reconciled?

Obviously, there are no easy answers to these loggerhead questions—and there will be none at all so long as the partners in the dialogue are unwilling to look beyond their respective "distinctive witnesses." But this can hardly be expected of them until they are ready to be led of the Spirit into broader perspectives in which they can view the universal mystery of the People of God, which is the Church. And they will never be ready for this until they have ventured out of their stereotyped views of themselves and of the other Christian traditions. For such projects of self-examination and exploration, the Golden Rule applies in a rather special way: as we would that others should outgrow their historic prejudices, so should we be ready to outgrow our own!

It so happens that Methodists have a special need for self-study in this connection because of our peculiar history. Methodism is a religious society that became a church without the complete loss of its character as a religious society. Methodists are not always mindful—and many non-Methodists not even aware—of this dual inheritance from both the Catholic *and* Protestant traditions in the Christian community, an experiment in the fusion of "justification by faith alone" with a disciplined ethic of "faith working by love." The history of this society-become-church is often confusing both to ourselves and to our neighbors. We are usually reckoned among the pietists—but no typically pietist group ever had anything like our *General Rules* and *Discipline*. We classify ourselves as Protestants, but none of the classical traditions of continental Protestantism had anything like the Wesleyan ideal of "Christian perfection" and the Wesleyan concept of evangelical morality. And yet, if the quintessential formula for ecumenism is something like "consensus in faith, community in worship, unity in mission," then it would be true to say that Methodism has been ecumenical from the very beginning. John Wesley was a rebel and a church reformer, a critic of the standing order, and a rude disturber of the false peace of Zion. Because he was convinced that the regular ministries of the Church of England were failing in their mission to the nation, he felt authorized by the Holy Spirit to raise up an irregular ministry of gospel proclamation and to organize a network of religious societies in England, Wales, Ireland—and later, America. To these he gave a distinctive set of "General Rules," a peculiar pattern of organization (classes, bands, etc.), a novel principle of lay-leadership, and a communal ethos that marked off the Methodists from the Nonconformists as well as from the "High Churchmen."

Despite all this, Wesley was no separatist. He never lifted a finger to overthrow the power structure of the Established Church nor even to invade it. The Methodists were ill-treated, but Wesley held them in the church and kept them loyal to the sacraments. The Anglican bishops reacted in varying degrees of distaste and bafflement, but they wisely refrained from any resort to formal excommunication in dealing with these Wesleyan irregulars. Wesley explains his notion of this strange relationship of society and church in terms that are highly relevant to our current situation in a remarkable essay entitled *Reasons Against a Separation* [of the Methodists] *From the Church of England* (1758):

Whether it be lawful or no (which itself may be disputed, being not so clear a point as some may imagine), it is by no means expedient for us to separate from the Established Church. . . .

10. Because the experiment has been so frequently tried already and the success never answered the expectation. God has, since the Reformation, raised up from time to time many witnesses of pure religion. If these lived and died (like John Arndt, Robert Bolton, and many others) in the churches to which they belonged, notwithstanding the wickedness which overflowed both the teachers and the people therein, they spread the leaven of true religion far and wide and were more and more useful till they went to Paradise. But if, under any provocation or consideration whatever, they separated and founded distinct parties, their influence was more and more confined; they grew less and less useful to others and generally lost the spirit of religion themselves in the spirit of controversy.

11. Because we have melancholy instances of this even now before our eyes. Many have in our memory left the church and formed themselves into distinct bodies — and certainly some of them from a real persuasion that they should do God more service. But have any separated themselves and prospered? Have they been either more holy or more useful than they were before?

12. Because by such a separation we should not only throw away the peculiar glorying which God has given us, . . . but should act in direct contradiction to that very end for which we believe God hath raised us up. The chief design in his providence in sending us out is, undoubtedly, to quicken our brethren, and the first message of all our preachers is to the lost sheep of the Church of England. Now, would it not be a flat contradiction to this design to separate from the Church? . . .

We look upon the Methodists (so-called) not as any particular party — this would exceedingly obstruct the grand

design for which we conceive God has raised them up —
but as living witnesses, in and to every party, of that Christianity which we preach. . . .

We are therefore debtors to all these, of whatever opinion
or denomination, and are, consequently, to do all that in us
lies . . . to the edification of the church.[1]

This self-image of an evangelical order within an inclusive
church was not effaced even when the Methodist societies
developed into separate churches with sacramental ministries of their own. Thus we learned—or might have
learned—that wide diversity within an inclusive fellowship
is not only tolerable but can actually be a vital service to
the cause of authentic unity. The early Methodists deliberately retained their direct ties with the ancient and
universal community but, quite as deliberately, they insisted on their freedom in Christian mission and nurture.
Wesley had no qualms in his use of laymen as preachers
in the Revival and as leaders of the societies. At the same
time, he refused, on principle, to allow these laymen to
administer the sacraments[2] which were available in the
Church of England. He even forbade Methodist preaching
services to be scheduled in competition with "church
hours." Given the violent and divisive spirit of the age,
this uneasy maintenance of the Methodist societies within
the unity of "Mother Church" is one of the most remarkable incidents in Protestant church history. When, however, the American Revolution had deprived the Methodists in the new republic of any ordained ministry for the
sacraments, Wesley proceeded—by his ordinations of

[1] Cf. John Wesley, Works, XIII, 225-28.

[2] Cf. John Wesley's sermon on "The Ministerial Office," Works, VII, 273-80.

Richard Whatcoat, Thomas Vasey, and Thomas Coke—
to remedy this defect himself rather than to approve the
pattern of sectarian self-ordination by laymen begun by
Philip Gatch and others at the Fluvanna Conference of
1779.[3]

The notion of the reunion of all Christians would
scarcely have crossed John Wesley's practical mind; in
eighteenth century Europe, it was unthinkable. Nevertheless, he cherished and tried to promote what he called
"the catholic spirit" in friend and foe alike. In his sermon
entitled "Catholic Spirit,"[4] he pleaded for his own version
of the distinction between the great basics of Christian
salvation (he was *not* an indifferentist!) and the range of
allowable opinions as to doctrine, liturgy, and polity. Given
the bare essentials of the gospel, "catholic spirit" incul-
cates liberty and charity in all else. In Wesley's view,
Christian unity ought naturally to include a spread of
diverse patterns and practices. The Body of Christ is always more deeply wounded by ill will than by variations
in thought and ceremony. Schism is the sign that Christian
love is dead, and when this happens, the restoration of the
external signs of unity is fruitless.[5]

For more than a half-century Wesley kept his movement on the course he had set for it and, naturally, hoped
that it would so continue after his death. In his very last
letter to America—to Ezekiel Cooper—he renewed this
plea:

[3] Cf. Emory S. Bucke (ed.), *The History of American Methodism* (New York:
Abingdon Press, 1964), I, 176-80. See also W. H. Fitchett, *Wesley and
His Century* (Nashville: Smith and Lamar, n.d.), pp. 266-67.

[4] Cf. Albert C. Outler (ed.), *John Wesley* ("A Library of Protestant
Thought"; New York: Oxford University Press, 1964), pp. 91-103.

[5] Cf. John Wesley's sermon, "On Schism," in *Works*, VI, 401-10.

See that you never give place to one thought of separating from your brethren in Europe. Lose no opportunity of declaring to all men that the Methodists are one people in all the world; and that it is their full determination so to continue,

> Though mountains rise, and oceans roll,
>
> To sever us in vain.[6]

But the fact was that the American Methodists had already taken the way of separation six years before, in 1784. The British Methodists experienced five years of turmoil after Wesley's death before their first schism broke wide open.[7] Thereafter in America and England, schism followed schism in controversy after controversy over a bewildering variety of issues: ecclesiastical authority, racial equality, lay representation, slavery, the status of the episcopacy, the doctrine of holiness, and many another. When the first "Ecumenical Methodist Conference" was held in London in 1881, there were ten separate denominations from the British side, eighteen from America— all Methodists![8]

Given this history, it is natural enough for Methodists to think first of unity in terms of the reunion of their own separated brethren. This is what the term "ecumenical" meant to us in the very first instance—and its usage, for the first pan-Methodist conference (1881), was an innovation among Protestants. The minutes of that first "ecu-

---

6 John Telford (ed.), *The Letters of the Rev. John Wesley* (London: Epworth Press, 1931), VIII, 260 (February 1, 1791).

7 Cf. W. J. Townsend, H. B. Workman & George Eayrs (eds.), *A New History of Methodism* (London: Hodder & Stoughton, 1909), I, 381-88, 488-502.

8 Cf. *Proceedings of the First Ecumenical Methodist Conference* (London: Phillips & Hunt, 1881).

menical" conference—and its successors—are highly in-
structive, for they reveal the tragic irony of Christians in
disarray on grounds that had little to do with *doctrine*.
The delegates were very much aware of their doctrinal
consensus[9] and they were awkwardly eager for "unity in
the Spirit." But their separate histories had estranged
them more deeply than their brave words admitted.[10] Yet
the bread of Christian fellowship cast upon ecumenical
waters is never wholly lost, and, as these conferences followed one another, their cumulative influence began to be
manifest. Out of these encounters came the impulses that
prepared Methodists for participation in trans-confessional
dialogue—at Edinburgh (1910) and thereafter—and the
Methodist initiatives for the formation of the United
Church of Canada (1925), the reunion of British Methodists in *The Methodist Church* (1932), the reunion of
three Methodist churches in America in a second *The
Methodist Church* (1939), the Church of South India
(1947), and other unions or reunions. In 1951, The
Ecumenical Methodist Council was formed to promote a
permanent program. In 1956 this became the World
Methodist Council, with a dual secretariat, dual head-
quarters, and dual archives for the British and American
sectors.[11]

[9] In the opening sermon Bishop Matthew Simpson declared, "There has been among the Wesleyan ranks no division as to doctrines. . . . All over the world Methodist theology is a unit." *Proceedings of the First Ecumenical Methodist Conference*, p. 17.

[10] Dr. Colin McKechnie professed to see "the hand of God in the divisions of Methodism. . . . Just as storms are designed to purify the atmosphere, so, in my humble opinion, have the various divisions of Methodism tended to purify us." *Proceedings of the First Ecumenical Methodist Conference*, pp. 53-54.

[11] Cf. Ivan Lee Holt and Elmer T. Clark, *The World Methodist Movement* (Nashville: The Upper Room, 1956).

This strong emphasis upon pan-denominational unity has, however, generated serious tensions among Methodists themselves and between Methodists and non-Methodist partners in the wider ecumenical movement. British Methodists, by and large, have tended to think and plan across "confessional" lines, particularly in their overseas connections—as in Canada, South India, Nigeria, etc. In England, they are deeply engaged in a complex process of negotiations with the Church of England for reunion on terms that entail decisive changes on both sides.[12] But American Methodism has not yet ventured any further than "consultations" with other Christians outside our family.[13] Many of us are convinced that the right order in ecumenical progress is to concentrate on the prior goal of "confessional unity" (unity of all the Methodists, all the Lutherans, Baptists, Presbyterians, Reformed, and other Protestant denominations) and *then* turn to the question of the whole Christian community, under conditions that would be more advantageous to all parties concerned, as they suppose. Others fear this approach, not only because it exempts us from commitment to unity projects closer to hand—in mission, in the community, etc. —but also because the pan-denominational principle (i.e., the union of all the branches of each denomination) is inconsistent with the premises of the New Delhi statement on unity, which looked toward the union of all Christians including Anglicans, Roman Catholics, and Orthodox, and for which the Methodist delegation voted.

---

12 See *Conversations Between the Church of England and the Methodist Church; A Report* (London: Epworth Press, 1963).

13 As, for example, in the current Consultation on Church Union; cf. George L. Hunt and Paul A. Crow, Jr. (eds.), *Where We Are in Church Union* (New York: Association Press, 1965).

In any case, Methodists have been actively engaged in all manner of ecumenical projects since Edinburgh (1910), and before. And, typically, our most important contribution has been *people*: Methodist men and women who have enlisted in the ecumenical cause and who have served it well. There was, preeminently, John R. Mott, of whom we have spoken. But Mott was ably seconded by many others, loyal churchmen as well as dedicated ecumenists: Frank Mason North and Harry Ward (architects of the Federal Council of Churches); Bishop Francis J. McConnell at Lausanne and Edinburgh; Bishop Ivan Lee Holt at Oxford, Edinburgh, Lund, and Evanston; Bishop G. Bromley Oxnam and Professor Clarence Tucker Craig at Amsterdam; Principal J. Newton Flew at Lund; Mr. Charles Parlin at New Delhi—and so the list might run on indefinitely. There has also been a notable number of Methodists in significant staff positions in the various ecumenical organizations and commissions.

At a second level, Methodism has provided substantial *financial support* for all the ecumenical projects in which it has been involved—except, curiously enough, the expenses of its own representatives in ecumenical commissions and conferences. Thus, Methodists who may have not felt personally involved in the ecumenical cause have, nevertheless, been aiding it indirectly.

At still a third level, Methodists have made another indirect but significant contribution to the spirit of ecumenism. We are, typically, the great pragmatists of the movement—not indifferent to, yet not readily preoccupied by, theological speculation. Nor are we heavily burdened by the weight of history. Our own liveliest memories (often recalled with more self-satisfaction than the facts warrant) cluster around our "success stories" in evangelistic outreach and conquest: the Methodist circuit rider on the American frontier, the Methodist missionaries at home and abroad. This triumphalist temper is, however, no more than the froth on our valid conviction (rooted in our origins) that the prime test of true doctrine is its fruitfulness in preaching, and the true measure of sound polity is its service to the Gospel. This was the genius of the Wesleyan revival and this is still the core of our evangelical tradition. But we have also sought to preserve our ties with the catholic traditions of "the Church of the Fathers." The "Message" of the uniting conference of the British Methodist Church made an emphatic point of this:

> The Methodist Church claims and cherishes its place in the Holy Catholic Church which is the Body of Christ. It rejoices in the inheritance of the Apostolic Faith and loyally accepts the fundamental principles of the historic creeds and of the Protestant Reformation. It ever remembers that in the Providence of God Methodism was raised up to spread Scriptural Holiness through the land by the proclamation of the Evangelical Faith and declares its unfaltering resolve to be true to its Divinely appointed mission.[14]

In both Britain and America "our present existing and established standards of doctrine"[15] were, by Mr. Wesley's

---

[14] Cf. Harold Spencer and Edwin Finch, *The Constitutional Practice and Discipline of the Methodist Church* (2d ed.; London: The Methodist Publishing House, 1958), p. 264.

[15] Emory Stevens Bucke (ed.), *Discipline of The Methodist Church: 1964* (Nashville: The Methodist Publishing House, 1964), Constitution, Sec. II, para. 9.1, p. 16. Cf. Spencer and Finch, *The Constitutional Practice and Discipline of the Methodist Church*, p. 264.

expressed design, grounded in the Anglican tradition of the *Homilies* and the *Articles of Religion* which, in their turn, had been carefully framed as an ecumenical bridge between the extremes of continental Protestantism and popery. By tradition, then, if not by conscious feeling, contemporary Methodism is genuinely "open" to serious dialogue with all the other church families in Christendom —heirs and debtors to them all, and yet also with a legacy to share with them.

Methodism's commitment to the ongoing ecumenical enterprise (national and global) has been reiterated numberless times in words and deeds over the years. Bishop Oxnam's Episcopal Address in 1948 (the year of the Amsterdam Assembly) was clear and emphatic:

> Methodism has co-operated in all the significant interdenominational endeavors, and rejoices in the privilege of sharing in the ecumenical fellowship. We should bear our fair share of the support of this Christian enterprise, contributing of our means and of our leadership and co-operating fully in all those measures that look to the extension of the Kingdom. . . . Methodism shared in the organization of the Federal Council of the Churches of Christ in America, and from the day of its charter membership to the present has been one of the co-operating Churches in this the most significant interdenominational endeavor in the nation.[16]

Bishop William C. Martin's Address in 1960 spelled this out more fully:

---

[16] Lud H. Estes (ed.), *Journal of the 1948 General Conference of The Methodist Church* (Nashville: The Methodist Publishing House, n.d.), pp. 163-64.

We believe in One Holy Catholic Apostolic Church and have always known ourselves to be within its fold. Not only do we believe in it but, with no boast of perfection, we lay claim to a record of commitment and participation that demonstrates our faith. For this we deserve no award of merit. It is part of our inheritance. . . .

This relationship [between denominationalism and ecumenism] is not ever easy to maintain. . . . Sometimes the question is raised in all sincerity, "Why is it necessary for Methodists, with our fellowship in a world-wide parish, to go outside our own denominational family for completeness of experience and Christian service?" The first reason why we must is that we cannot fulfill Christ's ministry to the world by ourselves. We must work with others. . . .

But there is a more profound reason for our continued participation in the ecumenical movement. It is the most dramatic and effective means by which we can declare our faith in the basic unity of the people of God . . . and can help to fulfill the prayer of our Lord that His disciples might all be one, "that the world may believe!" It is through our fellowship in the World Methodist Council, in various National Councils of Churches in many lands, and in the World Council of Churches that we can most competently make the distinctive contribution which we believe Methodism owes to the larger Church. . . .

At the same time, we are quite certain that our basic commitment to the Church universal is not incompatible with an enthusiastic loyalty to our own denomination. In fact, our only channel of service to the wider fellowship is through an actual existing denomination. Progress toward Christian unity will come not out of weakness but out of strength — from the deep conviction that the Church has a mission to fulfill of such magnitude that it calls all Christians to a common task and mission.[17]

This half-century of our continued participation in ecumenical study and service has had its own inevitable results in the subtle transformations that have become apparent in our self-understanding in the contemporary Christian community. As one reads the "proceedings" of the earlier Methodist Ecumenical Conferences (and our typical denominational "histories"), it is actually amusing to realize how stuffy and "triumphalist" was the atmosphere that the men who participated in them breathed without ever noticing it. Methodist superiority is not argued; it is announced as self-evident. The rest of Christendom is generally ignored, except for an occasional invidious comparison that, in the case of the Romans, amounted to the verdict of apostasy. Yet, decade by decade, the perspectives of these assemblies visibly widened and deepened; Methodist "triumphalism" has taken on more modest tones, and almost everywhere there is an increasingly vivid sense of our yeoman's rank in that

> . . . one great fellowship of love
> Throughout the whole wide earth.[18]

Methodism's openness to the ecumenical situation has coincided, accidentally, with a curious development in the evolution of theology in American Methodism—with consequences that are not altogether constructive for the cause

[17] Leon T. Moore (ed.), *Journal of the 1960 General Conference of The Methodist Church* (Nashville: The Methodist Publishing House, n.d.), pp. 192-94.

[18] John Oxenham, *Bees in Amber* (Oradell, N.J.: American Tract Society).

of ecumenical theology. By the turn of the present century, the doctrinal consensus of which Bishop Simpson had boasted in 1881 had been sadly shattered by a debilitating controversy over "holiness" and "entire sanctification," and by the first blows in the brawl between the fundamentalists and the modernists. The result was a real break in continuity with our rootage in the Wesleyan tradition. In reaction, Methodists turned their attention to the newer theological pacemakers who were translating the new ideas of European liberal Protestantism into the American idiom and church life. It makes an exciting half-century—from Walter Rauschenbusch to George Albert Coe to Harry Emerson Fosdick to Franklin N. Rall to Edgar S. Brightman; from the brothers Niebuhr to Paul Tillich to Karl Barth to Emil Brunner—and now to the "post-Bultmannian" exotics. Methodist scholars were in the thick of it all —with the majority of them trained in interdenominational theological centers, in this country or abroad, alongside colleagues from all the other Protestant traditions. The consequence is a veritable theological kaleidoscope, ecumenical rather more by accident than design, but richly representative of the entire spectrum of contemporary theology. But it has had an untoward and unintended side effect. In the process, the generality of Methodist scholars have lost their linkage with *the Wesleyan tradition* and are thus indisposed or ill-prepared for the crucial task of interpreting it to others at a time when it was never more relevant![19]

The basic core of the Methodist tradition is, of course, the common teaching of historic Christianity: the apostolic faith in the triune God—Creator, Redeemer, Con-

19 Cf. Albert C. Outler (ed.), *John Wesley*, pp. viii-ix, 26-33.

summator; in Jesus Christ as Lord and Savior to the glory of God the Father; in the Holy Spirit, the Lord and Giver of life; in the church catholic, whose mission is the edification of believers and the conversion of the world; in Christ's resurrection as the ground for our own hope of life here and hereafter. On these great themes—except for a revision here and there in their wording—the Methodist tradition is massive and clear. But in the *interpretation* of this common faith John Wesley bequeathed us a distinctive accent on the cardinal concept of *the grace of God* that has a peculiar relevance in the current ecumenical dialogue with both our Protestant and Catholic brethren, though for rather different reasons in each case. *Grace,* in the Wesleyan tradition, is *God's love-at-work,* in all its manifold ways in history and human existence. God is utterly free and sovereign; it follows, therefore, that his grace is also free and unmerited. But, by the same token, his human creatures were made to be free and responsible (able to respond) to God's loving initiatives in creation. This means that God's grace is "prevenient"—which reminds us that God must act before we *can* act, and that all our knowledge of God is of his love-in-action before and beyond our powers to manage it. God's grace is also "sustaining," even in the disorders which flow from our abuses of the grace of creation and the sin that corrupts our powers to live and to love. Grace is "saving"—which means that God in Christ has broken sin's damning power to shut us off from grace. By reopening the way from death to life, grace gives us a "grace-full" *future.* Grace brings "assurance"—the trusting heart may know God's pardoning love *directly.* Grace is "sacramental" but not *sacerdotal*—God's love is revealed to us in a myriad of "outward and visible signs" in all the gracious incidents of existence—but crucially and typically in the ritual symbols of birth and initiation (baptism and confirmation), and of nurture and maturation (Holy Communion). The effective "minister of grace" in *every* sacrament is God's Holy Spirit, who also gives to every event the quality of a sacramental occasion. Grace is "sanctifying"—for our acceptance of God's love sets us to the lifelong task of grateful and gracious living—which is what John Wesley meant by "Christian perfection!"[20] Thus grace becomes both the energy and the governor of the Christian's ethical enterprises in his service of God's righteous rule in human affairs. Grace, finally, is eschatological: life and death and resurrection are so many aspects of God's concern for us. This complex understanding of God's love has a wide-ranging significance for the problems of ecumenical theology. It illuminates many a dark corner in our mutual misunderstandings of revelation and faith, of conversion and nurture, of worship and work, of life in the Spirit and life in the Christian community. It opens a way between the "evangelical" and "catholic" traditions with its careful distinction between the *sacramental* and the *sacerdotal*.

In theory, at least, there is one other possible contribution which the Methodists have to make to the ecumenical dialogue. Who should know better than we that denominations may be justified in their existence for this "time being" or that, but not forever? We were commissioned by the Spirit of God "for the time being" to carry out an extraordinary mission of witness and service, for just so long as our life apart is effective in the economy of God's

---

[20] See Thomas S. Kepler (ed.), *Christian Perfection as Believed and Taught by John Wesley* (New York: The World Publishing Co., © 1954).

providence. We are, or ought to be, prepared to risk our life as a separate church and to face death as a denomination in the sure and lively hope of our resurrection in the true community of the whole people of God. As yet, neither the church we are, nor any of the churches that we know, constitutes that fullness of catholicity to which Christ called us in his prayer, "that *all* may be *one*." But the price of true catholicity may very well be the death and resurrection of the churches that we know—in the faith that God has greater things in store for his people than we can remember or even imagine. When will the churches be prepared to venture into the valley of *that* shadow of death, fearing no evil? Who can say? At the very least, however, the spiritual sons and daughters of John Wesley have less reason than most to doubt that faith may be careless of consequence for those who, "forgetting what lies behind and straining forward to what lies ahead, press on toward the goal for the prize of the upward call of God in Christ Jesus" (Phil. 3:13-14).

CHAPTER FIVE

OBSTACLES
ON THE WAY
TO UNITY

SOONER or later, even the zealot for Christian unity must face the shocking prospect that his cause may be ever so right and still turn out to be forlorn. This is "an age of ecumenism" and there are all too many churchmen who go about commending it who then visibly recoil from most of its obvious practical consequences, like the young Augustine with his cautious prayer: "Give me continence, but not yet."[1]

But even for those of us who fancy ourselves whole-heartedly committeed to our ecumenical concerns, there is the stark paradox that, although Christian unity is God's will for his people, it seems to lie far beyond any probable attainment in any foreseeable future. And this is, or ought to be, embarrassing. If we are serious in our ecumenical commitments, how are we to account for the continued estrangement of our churches in the face of the crises of our time? If Christians really *want* to get together, why don't they?

There is deep anguish in having to confess that our ardent wishes for unity are thwarted even as we wish them

---

[1] St. Augustine, *Confessions* 8.7 [17].

—and this from an inner conflict as well as the force of circumstances. Like Paul (cf. Romans 7:21-23), we see a sort of ecumenical war in the members of the Body of Christ. We delight in confessing that our unity in Christ is God-given; yet we halt and hesitate on the road that leads to this unity's actual realization. We are committed to the goal (e.g., the New Delhi statement on unity), but we seem to lack both the will and the wit to affirm the necessary practical means for the achievement of this goal.

Here, indeed, we are up against a vexed and baffling dilemma that has to be honestly faced and carefully probed —if only to learn the facts of ecumenical life and to prepare ourselves for the challenges and frustrations that lie ahead. Part of our resistance to God's manifest will for Christian unity must surely come from out of the dark mystery of evil itself. If God is calling his people to unity, the demonic powers are scarcely eager to be of any real help—for was it not the devil himself who invented the tactical slogan, "divide and conquer"?[2] But there is also a whole constellation of *visible* obstacles and complications that we can learn to recognize, appraise, and grapple with as part of our service to the cause of unity.

To begin with, there is a small cluster of anti-ecumenical prejudices shared by a great many Christians who fear the consequences of radical changes in traditions in which they feel themselves more or less at home. There is, for

[2] In 1891, at the second Methodist ecumenical conference, Dr. E. E. Hoss (later bishop) made this point rather trenchantly: ". . . when any Methodist denomination goes into a little village in which there is already a Methodist church of another denomination and builds a house and sends a pastor, it makes it absolutely unnecessary for the devil to be personally present in that village thereafter." [*Proceedings of the Second Ecumenical Methodist Conference* (New York: Hunt & Eaton, 1892), p. 128.] Why would not the same judgment hold in *interdenominational* rivalry?

example, what may be called *denominational narcissism*—
the powerful drive to ecclesiastical clannishness, reinforced
by pious feelings. It shows up in the contrast between our
sense of security within our denominational family—even
in its quarrels—and the strangeness we feel toward our
separated Christian brethren, especially when tensions
arise. The Roman Catholic version of this pious fascina-
tion with ourselves is called "triumphalism" and has been
roundly deplored in the Vatican Council. Among Protestants it often shows itself in the humble pride with which
we compare ourselves with others—and rarely in unfavor-
able terms. Thus denominational self-esteem and loyalty
get sadly confused and our impulses to risk very much for
unity are readily stifled.

A similar prejudice, which we have noted earlier (see
p. 3), is the powerful conviction—usually held by people
who stand to profit from it—that denominationalism is
God's providential arrangement for giving his church[es]
an optimum balance of unity and freedom. Why they
think it took Him so long to hit upon this clever design
they do not seek to explain, but they never fail to affirm
their thesis: if God is for denominationalism, who are we
to propose an alternative?

There is yet a third bias against ecumenism in which
malice is added to fear—which is as good a definition of
bigotry as any. For this, a sample will suffice to reveal a
mentality that is, alas, widespread enough to be tragically
mischievous:

> The most important issue facing the churches throughout the
> world today, so far as their future is concerned, is what is
> called the ecumenical movement. . . . The movement has as

its goal and purpose the development of the world church, or "the coming great church." The movement is described generally as "Christian unity." . . .

One of the most important qualifications of the great one-world church, when it comes into being, will be that it will suppress any opposition to its existence. It will be dictatorial and intolerant. . . .

At the heart of the entire ecumenical movement is a basic rejection of the Word of God as infallible and true. The Bible must take second place while the church organization moves up to the first place. . . .

What is so important just now is that Christian people should not help build this great church. They must see the corruption, the unbelief, the inclusivism, the apostasy that is involved. Thus they have a responsibility to help expose and oppose it in the name of the Lord. Moreover, they must help maintain churches that are true to the holy Scriptures and preach the everlasting Gospel of the grace of God.[3]

Besides these anti-ecumenical *prejudices*, one must also notice that there is a series of ecumenical *reservations*, legitimately felt by many advocates of unity, that must be reckoned with constructively in the further course of the dialogue. The first of these is the recognition that ecumenism is badly served by the "ecumaniacs" who extol unity for its own sake; who fling out irresponsible criticisms of their own denominations; who clamor for "instant ecumenism." The beginning of ecumenical wisdom is the frank admission that the obstacles in our way are real and

---

[3] Dr. Carl McIntire, *Men in a Hurry Building the One-World Church*, a pamphlet prepared and distributed by the 20th Century Reformation Hour, Collingswood, N.J.

rugged, that our laggard pace is not merely the fault of misguided souls who lack *our* vision. With the best will in the world, our further progress is bound to be uneven and, without great patience and wisdom, ecumenical zeal can do more harm than good.

Some of us may also need a caution against "indifferentism" to which we may succumb in our impatience with all the stubborn haggling over doctrinal questions that seem of minor importance to some of us. There are all too many amiable souls who have the eager, shallow notion that these doctrinal questions are matters of *taste,* which may be tolerated without being resolved.

It cannot be stressed too strongly that the only conceivable unity worth having will express the full integrity of our respective convictions as to what really is true in the Christian message. If we are ever to come to honest consensus, it will be as the result of prolonged exposure to real issues in conscientious debate—and this in an atmosphere of dignity and mutual respect where the goal is persuasion, not conquest. All veteran ecumenists have come to take this for granted.

A third factor that slows our progress toward unity comes from the discouraging evidence that ecumenical organizations are all too easily dominated by their own provisional arrangements for getting their business done. Every institution must perforce have bureaus and bureaucrats to administer policy and facilitate the programs of cooperative work. But what has happened in all too many cases (as in the National Council of Churches and the World Council of Churches) is that executive officers— often because of a default by member churches—come to *make* policy and administer it, too. Moreover, this tendency does not depend on the size of the institution but on its character—on the ease with which loosely federated or international bodies tend to create power vacuums which are inevitably filled by the bureaucrats.[4] No plan of union will be worth the risks involved unless its basic constitution provides for the careful limitation of executive power by a system of inbuilt checks and balances, which will include a due process of appeal by referendum.

So much, then, for the prejudices that plague us and the cautions that warn us against unrealistic hopes. But even if the prejudices were purged and the cautions duly observed, there is still a whole phalanx of basic, substantive issues that divide the churches with no easy agreement in sight. They cannot be dismissed; they must not be minimized, and no amount of brotherly love will exempt us from the protracted agony of mind and heart in store for those who are seriously concerned with an honest consensus. And yet, without such a consensus, there is no ground for meaningful unity. Ecumenical realism, therefore, demands that we tackle these issues, not merely as obstacles but also as challenges.

One way of identifying the first of these issues is by noticing the tension between those who stress agreement in some doctrinal "confession" as the precondition for community and those who stress *community* as the prior context within which doctrinal consensus can be sought thereafter. The former assume that there is *one system of Christian truth* lodged somewhere—in the Bible, in church tradition, or in *their* church's "confession"!—and that assent to this system of "pure doctrine" is the mini-

---

4 Cf. Keith R. Bridston and Walter D. Wagoner (eds.), *Unity in Mid-Career; An Ecumenical Critique* (New York: The Macmillan Co., 1963), pp. 30-45.

mum price of genuine unity. There are others who are impressed by the fact that the Christian community began with an *event in history*—God in Christ—and that the bare acknowledgment of this event ("Jesus Christ is Lord") created a fellowship that then proceeded to develop its necessary forms of liturgy, discipline, and doctrine. The early church had no canon, no creed, no single polity, and no single system of doctrine. Yet its sense of Christocentric community was so strong that it survived a succession of severe crises, evolving in each crisis such new patterns (canon, creed, and hierarchy) as were required.

Medieval and Protestant Christianity took a different tack by insisting on *doctrinal conformity* as the condition of community and by making doctrinal dissent the valid ground for excommunication. To this it added the use of force: to compel assent or to punish dissent. This led straightway to intolerable conflict when rival parties emerged with conflicting systems of "pure doctrine" and with contradictory patterns of liturgy and polity, each declared to be guaranteed by divine authority. When conscientious men, possessing infallible systems, stand in conflict over against each other, their prospects of honest consensus are nil. The alternative—a desperate one for any old-line "confessionalist"—is to admit that *the* Christian truth is *not* a set of *propositional truths,* nor *any* conceptual formulation, but JESUS CHRIST, known in the encounter of faith that is generated by the Holy Spirit. The original Christ-Event created the original Christian community. And, as this Event is re-presented in the church through the preaching of the Word (i.e., Jesus Christ) and the administration of the sacraments (i.e., the effective symbols of the real presence and action of Jesus Christ in the congregation of the faithful), so also is the Christian community renewed and given the right and the power to celebrate the Christ-Event in worship and to interpret it doctrinally.

The modern ecumenical movement has been made possible by the recovery of the sense that, just as theology is "faith seeking an intelligent self-understanding" (Anselm), so also doctrinal consensus emerges in the Christian *community* as it seeks to understand the Event which called it forth and continues to renew its life. When one group of Christians stands apart from another until there is agreement on some existing confession or code, there can be no vital community. When, however, the two groups discover and acknowledge their basic, God-given *community in Christ,* they are then in a position to grapple with their theoretical differences in the only kind of atmosphere that gives promise of real progress toward consensus.

Another cardinal issue that the ecumenical dialogue has forced into the center of our enterprise is the question of *authority in the church.* All Christians deny any ultimate authority to human reason or feeling; all appeal to God's self-revelation as the ground of our knowledge of God's grace and of his will in the world. But how do we come by this divine revelation and what are we to make of it? How is revelation, however come by, rightly interpreted and applied in controversial cases? Here is where the roads fork. Protestants have held traditionally to the prime authority of Holy Scripture as containing

all things necessary to salvation; so that whatsoever is not read therein, nor may be proved thereby, is not to be required of any man that it should be believed as an article of faith, or be thought requisite or necessary to salvation.[5]

Roman Catholics, at least since the Council of Trent, have generally held to a *two*-source theory of revelation: the *Bible,* as the constitutive deposit of Christian truth, and *Tradition,* as the interpretive action of the church in determining what Scripture means. Where Scripture is obscure, Protestants normally appeal to the whole of the biblical message or to their denominational "confession." For the Roman Catholics, it is the *magisterium* (teaching authority) of the church that is decisive and, within that *magisterium,* the court of last resort is the Bishop of Rome.

In recent years, Protestants have begun to recognize the omnipresence of tradition in their various interpretations of Scripture; during the same period, Roman Catholics have become increasingly involved in a lively study of the Bible as the primary norm by which to judge their traditions. But neither Scripture *nor* tradition, nor Scripture *and* tradition add up to the Christian's full measure of authority. Beyond and behind them both lies the mystery of God's gift of the Holy Spirit in the "I-thou" encounters of authentic Christian experience. "Private judgment" is a misleading phrase; yet the free assent of heart and mind has to be the final touchstone of authority in religion—in the sense that the objectively right must be subjectively affirmed before it is truly authentic. On the other hand, what is often put forward as private *judgment* is too often more "private" than it is an informed "judgment," and so falls into error.

---

[5] Emory Stevens Bucke (ed.), *Discipline of The Methodist Church: 1964,* Articles of Religion, V; para. 65, p. 37.

All of this would suggest that any ecumenically significant doctrine of authority must be composite: it must combine the primacy of the deposit of revelation in Scripture with the experience of the church evolved in the Christian tradition—and both these held together in our hearts and heads as we seek to hear the Word of God in Scripture and to *think with the church*. Obviously, a great deal more study and discussion in this area is called for before the churches can formulate even the rudiments of an adequate doctrine of authority for ecumenical dialogue. It should be noted, however, that the Roman Catholics have made a crucial advance in their consideration of this problem in their decree *On Divine Revelation*. This has reopened the question of Scripture and Tradition for fresh study and discussion within the Catholic Church and also between Catholics and Protestants.

A third area of formidable confusion among Christians is the manner and meaning of valid *worship*. Here we touch the lifeblood of the church, for all Christians agree that faith's first fruit is the celebration of God's grace in *corporate* worship, in one form or another. But by what forms—or how many? All Christians agree that *insin*-cerity in the sanctuary cancels the validity of *any* form of worship—but it is equally clear that sincerity by itself does not validate any form, either. Here we have a highly sensitive and tangled problem with an unhappy history that has generated far more heat than light. Some Christians are deeply attached to set forms in their corporate worship—and their private devotions as well. Others believe that such forms quench the Spirit. Anglicans have a single ritual for their "Morning Prayer" and Holy Communion while the Roman Catholics have several—

albeit with the Roman rite predominant. In the Protestant house there are many rituals—good, bad, and improvised—but no consented principle for choosing between them. This proliferation of ritual practice has forced us away from any doctrinaire insistence on one inflexible pattern as the model for *all*. But various modes of worship must have a *common meaning* in their depths—and it is this meaning that must be groped for in the course of our growth toward authentic Christian community.

One point, however, should be made even now about our confusions in forms of worship. Somewhere along the line our quarreling forefathers lost sight of the vital distinction between *liturgy* and *ritual*—and we have long since so blurred them together that we use them now as synonyms. This was, and still is, a disaster. Liturgy is the *ordered act of worship,* in any of its ritual *forms.* Liturgy is our part in that divine-human interaction in which the Holy Spirit takes an *aggregation* of "strangers" and transforms them into a *congregation* of brothers and sisters in the Lord. Liturgy is what Christians *do* to participate in this true miracle of spiritual transformation. The various *visible* forms of this liturgical action in the church constitute *ritual.* In the nature of the case, therefore, there is no one ritual form (ceremony) that is invariably appropriate —and none at all that makes the liturgical act occur. By the same token, however, there can be no worship (liturgy) without some ritual form; for even the "silence" of a Quaker meeting or the hearty informality of a "brush arbor" revival have their ceremonial elements. Thus, the crucial ecumenical question about worship is not whether it should be "formal" or "informal," but how its essence (adoration) can best be related to its form (ceremonies) without confusing the two. Here again, we are on the way toward consensus, but it is not imminent—and the pace of progress cannot be forced.

A fourth issue that still looms large in all our discussions turns on the meaning of the Gospel and the appropriate means of communicating it. All Christians agree that the heart of the Gospel is the good news that God in Christ has taken away our sins and has saved us from the powers of sin and death. But from there on, the problems of interpretation mount, and so do the disagreements. There are those who insist on the radical difference between the Gospel of God in Christ and the message of salvation in all the other religions of mankind; they also stress the radical discontinuity between Christianity and Judaism, between the Old and the New Testaments. Again, there are those who account for Christianity's minority situation in the world as divinely intended. Others are convinced that the only limits to God's saving grace are those set by the failure of Christians in their mission and by the hard hearts of those who "hear" the Gospel and go on unheeding. Protestants tend to deny the reality of "natural religion"; Catholics incline toward the view that the revelation of God in Christ is the *climax* of his valid self-revelations in *all* religions—made before, and even apart from, the Incarnation of the Word of God in Christ. What Protestants fear above all is man's inveterate bent to idolatry (the heathen confusion of creature and Creator). Catholics have an opposite anxiety, that the universal outreach of God's love not be minimized or too narrowly constricted.

Christians are also in honest disagreement as to the appropriate modes and media for the communication of the Gospel. There are many who will contend, not only for "the *faith* . . . once for all delivered to the saints," but also for the first century language in which that faith was first delivered, or else for some sixteenth or eighteenth century translation of that language. Others, hypersensitive to the radical differences between modern scientific world views and the prescientific views naturally present in the Bible, are passionately determined to "de-mythologize" the Scriptures in order to make them more "relevant" in our contemporary Christian witness. There are many Christians who believe that in the communication of the Gospel we must depend upon "the reasonableness of Christianity" as its prime commendation to modern men. Others draw back from such a notion as a sign of *un*faith because, as they believe, unless the preaching of the Gospel is an offense to human minds, it does not amount to that "foolishness of preaching" by which "it pleased God . . . to save them that believe" (I Cor. 1:21, KJV). Here, as elsewhere, there are deep cleavages to be bridged.

We come, finally, to the prickliest of all the ecumenical nettles—the cluster of problems that goes by the fancy term *ecclesiology,* which is the doctrine of the church and, specifically, the proper terms of its membership and ministry. The vast majority of Christians confess "one holy catholic and apostolic church"—and then fall into profound disagreement as to what this really means. What is worse, our disagreements tend to spin off into a series of either/or disjunctions. The unity of the church is either "visible" *or* "invisible"—but which? Its "holiness" is either "sacral" (inhering in the visible sacraments) *or* "eschatological" (related to the Holy Spirit's presence in the church, both here and hereafter). The catholicity (universality) of the church is found either in its inclusive fellowship of all professed Christians *or* else in the remnants[6] of "the true believers," here and there, now and then (i.e., as a divine event but not a historical continuity). The *apostolicity* of the church depends either on "the historic episcopate" in unbroken succession from the apostles *or* else on the succession of apostolic truth accepted as traditional by the community as a whole, from age to age. The mission of the church is focused either on evangelism *or* on social Christianity.

Now, the fatal flaw in such disjunctive arguments is "the fallacy of negative inference." This happens when the two halves of an either/or proposition are not really exclusive. Thus, when you affirm one, you negate the other *by inference* though not in fact. This disjunction implies that if the church is "visible," then it cannot be "invisible." But all Christian experience testifies to the fact that the church is *both* visible *and* invisible, in various aspects and relations. The only way to avoid the false conclusions of these either/or arguments is to translate the valid points they are concerned with into *other* propositions—and talk about the sense in which the church *is,* and should be, visible in human society, and the other sense in which it is truly invisible ("the communion of saints," etc.). So also with the other disjunctions. The church is both holy *and* secular, catholic *and* evangelical; apostolic in its history *and* in its message—but, in each case, in a different sense —and these complex relations need to be sorted out.

There is a final problem that we must mention here and it is one on which we have made almost no real progress since we first dared to broach it at Edinburgh (1937): the terms of the church's membership and ministry. Who

6 See Isaiah 10:21-22; 11:11; 37:31; 46:3.

rightly "belongs" to the church? Who may rightly administer her sacraments? Christians may quarrel about many things and still maintain fellowship. But when they dispute each other's church membership or valid ministry, they are already separated—and this has been the most fruitful source of schism in church history.

All Christians believe that church membership is somehow linked with baptism—but what does baptism mean? Who is eligible for the sacrament? What is its proper mode of administration? Thus far, none of these questions has been answered to the satisfaction of all the parties in the ecumenical dialogue. Again, all Christians agree that the Lord's Supper is the quintessence of the means of grace. But what "happens" at the Table of the Lord; who is eligible to partake; who may rightly administer the Supper —and by what rite(s)? Here, too, we have long been at loggerheads. Inside these tangles, however, there is still another—the knottiest of them all. It is the problem of order and ordination. All Christians are agreed that baptism and confirmation constitute some kind of an ordination of a person to the general priesthood of all believers— the People of God.[7] This "People"—the laity—*is* the church's visible presence in the world.[8] But it is also generally agreed that it belongs to the good order of the church that, from this general priesthood, there should be called out and selected a representative ministry (*clerus*), chiefly for the administration of the sacraments and the pastoral direction of the People (*laos*)—"to equip God's people for their mission in the upbuilding of Christ's Body

---

[7] Cf. I Peter 2:5, 9-10. See also Clifford W. Edwards, *Christian Being and Doing* (Cincinnati: Service Center, 1966).

[8] Cf. Chapter IV of Vatican II's *Constitution On the Church* for a similar doctrine of the apostolate of the laity.

92

in the world"⁹ (Eph. 4:12). It is further agreed that the qualifications for any such representative ministry must include both a personal vocation ("call") and an objective judgment by responsible church leaders that the person selected has the requisite gifts and graces to represent the *whole* church in any of its local manifestations (but preeminently in the administration of the sacraments).

Now come the questions—and the conflicting answers. How is this representative character conferred so that the historic continuity of the church is safeguarded? There are those who insist that this can be done only by bishops who stand in unbroken temporal succession from the first apostles. This, clearly, would be a neat and orderly arrangement, but it has the flaw of being unproved *historically*—and also of being in dispute within those churches claiming that each of them has such an episcopate. There are other possible solutions: continuity of ministerial order through the succession of "presbyters" (elders)—with or without "bishops," as in the case of Methodists, Lutherans, and Presbyterians. Still others insist that, since the local congregation is the basic unit of church life and government, all necessary continuity is provided by the congregation in the light of its knowledge of the succession of the apostolic truth, which does not require a historic continuity of transmission!

There are two obvious requirements in the polity of any well-ordered Christian community—unity *and* liberty— but then the disagreements break out as to how both can be secured, and in what relation. Unity requires some sort of *connectional* polity and some pattern of regularity;

⁹ Author's translation.

liberty demands a range of choices and, therefore, pluralism. We already have liberty, of a sort, in our present situation—and this is what many of us cherish in it. If we should also choose unity, would we lose this cherished liberty?

The test case for this agonizing question is the problem of ministerial order—how could we reunite the ministries of our divided churches, even if we wanted to do so? And this gets us, finally, to the triple-center of the ecumenical problem: *re*-baptism, *re*-confirmation, *re*-ordination. Even now, instances are not infrequent where converts to Rome or Byzantium or Canterbury (the Roman Catholic, the Orthodox, or the Episcopal confessions)—or to the Baptists and Disciples!—are "re-baptized." Whatever explanation these communions may offer for re-baptism, there is no avoiding the fact that it involves some sort of denial of previous baptism, on the grounds either of mode or administration. But the mutual recognition of "separated brethren" as Christians implies the recognition of the validity of their baptism. Thus, re-baptism is an ecumenical monstrosity. The first step toward a reunited ministry must be a firm agreement that it will *not* involve re-baptism or even "conditional" baptism.

But what then can be done about re-confirmation? The Orthodox, the Romans, and the Anglicans still insist on confirmation (*re*-confirmation!) and this implies that non-Catholic confirmands are not recognized by them as having been authentic *members* of the church up to this point. This is not only intolerable but false. On similar grounds, these Catholic churches also insist on the re-ordination of non-Catholic ministers which would mean, for us, the repudiation of those ministerial orders that we have received and exercised, imperfectly, to be sure, but in good faith and not without the blessings of God. Many Protestants (but not all!) could be brought to the agreement that *all* our separated ministries (including the Orthodox, Roman, and Anglican) are *historically* "irregular" in one degree or another in the sense that, somewhere along the line, there have been lapses of one sort or another that broke (or tainted) the strictly "regular" *historical* continuity. But none of us, I take it, is prepared to deny that these "irregular" orders are valid in their good essence—since we, and others, can testify that they have been graciously honored, in their use, by the "gifts" and the "fruit" of the Holy Spirit.

Thus, re-confirmation and re-ordination are simply unthinkable in a general formula for reunion. What then? There have been several suggestions for "services of mutual reconciliation" of our disparate ministerial orders, in which representatives of all parties would lay hands on each other and leave the Holy Spirit to determine what had happened. The most that can be said for such schemes is that they would produce *amiable* confusion—but this would soon enough turn to a jangling when somebody made the claim that such services had constituted re-ordination after all—and who doubts that this would happen? It would seem, therefore, that the only feasible procedure—if ever some version of an episcopal polity is agreed to by all—would be to enroll *all* the certified ministers of the uniting churches in the clergy of the united church forthwith—and then go on from there with *subsequent* confirmations and ordinations by the bishops of the united church. This would, indeed, make a problem for the Catholics, for it would be a deliberate breach in the continuity of the laying on of hands. On the other side, it would be a major mutation for most Protestants. This is why the bare mention of such proposals stirs feelings that warn us that we are not yet even within striking distance of any quick and easy solution.

If we look at this whole picture against its tragic background and reckon the results of the ecumenical movement against that background, they are indeed impressive. But if we refocus the same picture against the swirling foreground of world history—where the churches are and where their mission is cast—and then face these obstacles that stand between us and our goal, even the optimists have their moments of genuine despair. The ecumenical good we are pledged to do—and could have done—still goes undone, and the ecumenical "evil" that we have often inveighed against in our pronouncements continues, unmitigated by all our self-justifying explanations. Here, as in our own personal dilemmas, we are faced with the grim predicament that, much as we may delight in the ideal of unity in our hearts, we are also enmeshed in historically-conditioned situations that threaten to thwart our best efforts and highest hopes.

But it is just such realism that could open our ears to the redeeming word that came to Paul. What we as men cannot do, God can do with us, if we are truly trustful. Only God can open the way around these obstacles that block ecumenical union. Only prayer and openness to his will can open that way or lead us in it. Our part in the project is to ratify our commitment to the cause of Christian unity. It is for the ablest minds among us to wrestle with these problems and to struggle for adequate answers. It is for the generality of Christians to prepare their hearts and wills for the changes and confusions that are bound to come along as we move forward. But none should forget that it is *God's* grace and providence that has wrought such progress as we have seen thus far and that our only valid prayer for further progress is that it shall be as God wills it. Mott and Temple planted; Oxnam and John XXIII have watered—and others with them. But it is God who has given the increase and who will bring us into the *fullness* of that community, the promise of which we are already beginning to know.

CHAPTER SIX

CHRISTIAN
COMMUNITY
BEGINS AT HOME

IN THE early days ecumenism was a minority movement, led by a handful of pioneers, supported by a remnant in the churches. It was, in fact, a project of individuals who were, indeed, loyal churchmen, but who were not able to commit their respective denominations to much more than benevolent interest in their cause. To be sure, the great world conferences made something of a splash, but they were spaced apart on the calendar and left the vast majority of church folk untouched. It was almost as if the cause of Christian unity were the hobby of a pious fraternity who had found a novel formula for combining their avocations: Christian unity, tourism, and photography! John R. Mott was almost certainly the most widely traveled public figure in the first half of the twentieth century (first as President of the World YMCA's, later as President of the World Council of Churches). Halford Luccock of Yale, who had known Mott for many years, used to josh him about "the ecumenical Rover Boys"—which was more than a hint of a feeling, widely shared, that all this ecumenical tourism was well-intentioned but practically futile.

There has always been much hopeful talk about "ecumenicity at the grass roots," but nothing much ever came of it. The ecumenists were not often the movers and shakers in their own denominations and the men who ran the churches did not have much surplus time or energy for ecumenical affairs. In the rhetoric of the ecumenical conferences there has been a standard formula: that this report or that resolution "be accepted by this conference and transmitted to the churches for study and appropriate action." This is always voted, and, all too soon forgotten. Bishop Angus Dun's comment about the Episcopal Church would apply to others: "There is an ecumenical interest in our church, but it is a sideshow—not under the main tent." Even the word "ecumenical" is sometimes grumbled at, by people who have no difficulty with other polysyllables—like "denominational."

Gradually, however, this gap between the ecumenical coterie and the leadership of the churches has been closing —with something of a rush in the last few years. In 1955, in preparation for the Oberlin Conference (1957), Professor Paul Minear organized a network of regional "faith and order" study groups across the continent. In the course of eighteen months this engaged more people in significant ecumenical study and debate than had been involved in the previous half century. It also helped to make the Oberlin Conference the most successful of its kind since Edinburgh (1910). And now the Second Vatican Council has spread a new kind of interest in ecumenism throughout the Roman Church and far beyond as well. Protestant denominations now have commissions on ecumenical affairs; most seminaries have courses in ecumenics; most churches have special ecumenical services.

All this means, among other things, that the ecumenical movement is finally moving up to its last frontier: the local community. The cause of unity has finally become too interesting and urgent to be left to the professionals. And this is the cue for the *churches* to bestir themselves and to provide more vigorous and creative leadership in the movement than most of them have done to date, and for the church folk generally to make the cause of unity their own cause. We are at the point where "do-it-yourself ecumenism" is not merely a pert phrase. Unless what it stands for begins to manifest itself in local congregations and communities, the whole future of the ecumenical movement will be in jeopardy.

This is why we made the unity statement, formulated at New Delhi (1961), turn on the phrase "all in each place." We wanted to make sure that unity was anchored in the local community—all the Christian people in a given *locus,* in all their variety of denomination, race, politics, and social and economic class:

19. The place where the development of the common life in Christ is most clearly tested is in the local situation, where believers live and work. There the achievements and the frustrations are most deeply felt: but there too the challenge is most often avoided. It is where we live and work together daily that our Lord's own test is most clearly imposed, 'by this shall all men know that ye are my disciples, if ye have love one to another'. . . .

20. (a) There is need for an increase in opportunities of growing together as local churches; through common worship, Bible study groups, prayer cells, joint visitation, common witness in our communities. Locally as in the whole ecumenical

movement we should be especially ready in Christian love to seek out and to establish fellowship with those traditions and minorities to which we are not now related. . . .

21. (b) Ordinary social life already brings men together into various associations — academic, professional, industrial, political, etc. Within these forms of unity there is need for a Christian unity of those who may learn from each other how to bear their witness in those settings. . . . Denominational divisions are often found to be quite irrelevant on this frontier.[1]

This is sound doctrine—and yet, like many another notion hatched at these international conferences, this vision of local ecumenism has still to be glimpsed in many cities and towns across the country. Christian community begins at home—which is to say that, as yet, it has hardly begun. Thus, the greatest challenge and opportunity before us in ecumenism is *to step up the pace of encounter and study* in as many local situations as possible, and everywhere *to pass from encounter and study to ecumenical action.*

Ecumenism at the local level is no more properly concerned with Christian unity as an end in itself than it is, or should be, at national and world levels. Here, as everywhere else, the ecumenical imperative is mission: Christian unity in order that the world may believe. This means that Christians must move out of their churches into the world *together* with a *common* word of gospel and pardon from God to man, a *united* witness of God's judgment against man's inhumanity to man, and a *united* offer of effective service to men and women in their actual needs.

But the obvious first step is for the Christians "in each

[1] *The New Delhi Report,* pp. 122-23.

place" to get acquainted. It is as simple—and as difficult —as that. In commenting on the "Malines Conversations," Cardinal Mercier said this memorably: "In order to be united, we must love one another; in order to love one another, we must know one another; in order to know one another, we must meet one another."[2]

But most of us know by now that random and unplanned meetings between even well-intentioned souls are awkward and self-conscious. When neither group knows enough of the other's background to ask the right questions or to understand the answers that are offered, very little can happen. This means that before such meetings, provision should be made for each participating group to be competently briefed on the distinctive features of the other.

Let me list three examples of how this has worked. For the 1965 "Octave of Christian Unity," the student leaders at Southern Methodist University and the University of Dallas (Roman Catholic) planned a joint service of prayer, hymns, Bible readings (plus *two* short sermons). In preparation for this, the Catholics invited one of the Protestant chaplains to interpret to them the Protestant position—and to field their questions about Protestantism. Similarly, the Protestants invited the Catholic chaplain to present the Catholic position. As a result, this was one of the most fully effective services of worship I have ever witnessed.

A second example comes from a St. Louis suburb where neighboring Methodist and Episcopalian parishes have been "explaining themselves" to each other in a series of parish "forums."

[2] Samuel McCrea Cavert, *On the Road to Christian Unity*, p. 134.

My third example shows what can happen when *a dedicated individual* takes the initiative in promoting mutual understanding between separated Christians. In Madison, Wisconsin, there is a Dominican nun, Sister M. Suzanne, O.P., who is a schoolteacher. She became so earnestly concerned that Roman Catholics should be well-prepared for their newly-encouraged encounters with Protestants that she undertook (with appropriate consultation) the development of a film strip, *A Foundation for Dialogue*,[3] that tells the essential story of each of the major churches in America through suitable pictures and a "narration" that is remarkably accurate and appreciative. Here is "do-it-yourself ecumenism" at its best—a sort of one-woman-ecumenical-movement! She has kindly given permission to quote from the section on the Methodists, below:

SLIDE 145 — DOVE

NARRATION *(chorus):* O, for a thousand tongues to sing / my great Redeemer's praise, / The glories of my God and King, / the triumphs of His grace.

SLIDE 146 — JOHN WESLEY

NARRATION: When John Wesley, an Anglican priest, began the Methodist movement in the eighteenth century, his driving concern was that the Established Church of England had seemingly forgotten its mission to the poor.

SLIDE 147 — SLUMS

NARRATION: To these poor—the debtors, the coal-miners, the men on the wharves and in the fields—he preached a gospel of simple trust and energetic dedication.

3 See "Recommended Materials," p. ix.

SLIDE 148 — MAN AT PRAYER

NARRATION: He taught the personal love and care of God for every man — a love and care which a man experiences through the witness of the Holy Spirit within him, and which draws him to commit himself completely to Christ.

SLIDE 149 — NEIGHBORHOOD HOUSE

NARRATION: This commitment to Christ is the core of the Methodist understanding of Christian perfection.

SLIDE 150 — 2ND NEIGHBORHOOD HOUSE

NARRATION: The presence of Christ, loving and loved, so transforms a man and his actions that his love, like God's, will go out to all, especially where the need is greatest.

SLIDE 151 — PASTOR IN LIBRARY

NARRATION: The Methodist Church does not profess any specific confession, or statement of beliefs, but its life and thought are guided by the Bible, the Fathers of the Church, and its own Book of Discipline.

SLIDE 152 — CONGREGATION

NARRATION: The Methodist's religious life is centered in his local church. However, no congregation is completely independent or autonomous, but is connected with the rest of the denomination through Annual Conferences and through the General Conference.

SLIDE 153 — PASTOR VISITING PARISHIONERS

NARRATION: The Pastor's duties in the parish to which he is appointed are to instruct the people in the Scriptures; to administer doctrine, the sacraments, and the Discipline; to visit his parishioners In their homes.

SLIDE 154 — DIRECTOR OF EDUCATION

NARRATION: Women play a very active role in Methodist life. They may be engaged in the work of the Church as ministers, or deaconnesses, or in a score of other functions, especially educational.

SLIDE 155 — BAPTISMAL FONT

NARRATION: The first of the two sacraments recognized by Methodists is Baptism.

SLIDE 156 — 2ND BAPTISMAL FONT

NARRATION: There is no reference in the ceremony to Original Sin, since this is not seen as any form of guilt which would require remission. The sacrament is understood rather as a sign of faith and a symbol of God's merciful acceptance.

SLIDE 157 — PRESENTATION OF CHILD

NARRATION: When an infant is baptized, the entire congregation becomes responsible for his Christian education.

SLIDE 158 — CHILDREN'S CLASS

NARRATION: After Baptism, he is enrolled as a preparatory member of the congregation. When he is old enough, he will make his own decision to accept full membership.

SLIDE 159 — CONFIRMATION

NARRATION: On the day of his Confirmation, the young Methodist formally declares his faith in Christ, his belief in Scripture as the Word of God, and his allegiance to the Methodist Church.

SLIDE 160 — CONFIRMATION

NARRATION: He is now fully a member of his congregation, and begins to share more completely in its life and worship.

SLIDE 161 — CONGREGATION AND CHOIR

NARRATION: Although Methodist worship may take many forms, it will always include readings from Scripture, prayer, preaching, and the singing of hymns. John Wesley and his brother Charles left their followers a heritage of more than six thousand hymns.

SLIDE 162 — ELEMENTS

NARRATION: The sacrament of the Lord's Supper is celebrated at least four times a year.

SLIDE 163 — MINISTERS BEFORE TABLE

NARRATION: The Book of Discipline describes this sacrament as "not only a sign of the love that Christians ought to have among themselves, one to another, but rather [also] a sacrament of our redemption by Christ's death."

SLIDE 164 — RECEPTION

NARRATION: "The body of Christ," continues the Discipline, "is given, taken, and eaten in the Supper, only after a heavenly and spiritual manner. And the means whereby the body of Christ is received and eaten in the Supper is faith."

SLIDE 165 — PEOPLE LEAVING CHURCH

NARRATION: Important as worship is to the Methodist, his commitment can never stop at the church doors. Since the days of Wesley, Methodism has always been a religion of social concern.

SLIDE 166 — PRESS

NARRATION: The Methodist Publishing House is a good example of this social concern.

SLIDE 167 — PERIODICAL DISPLAY

NARRATION: In its role as publisher, printer, and distributor, the Publishing House plays a large part in informing Methodists of the social stance of the Church.

SLIDE 168 — POLITICIAN

NARRATION: By the social creed of his Church, every Methodist is committed to the betterment of the society in which he lives, no matter what his position in that society may be.

SLIDE 169 — PUBLIC SCHOOL

NARRATION: For this reason Methodists prefer to be involved in the public school system, rather than in any system of private schools.

SLIDE 170 — PRINCIPAL, PARENTS, CHILD

NARRATION: They believe that "it is possible for public school teachers, without violating the traditional American principle of separation of church and state, to teach moral principles and spiritual values."

SLIDE 171 — CITY VIEW

NARRATION: John Wesley claimed the world as his parish, and the whole world has always been the concern of Methodists, in social reform, in civic life, and today especially in efforts toward Christian unity. While they recognize all Christian groups as belonging equally to the one

Church of Christ, they strive with all of them for an ever deeper and more authentic unity.

How many Methodists could describe themselves as faithfully—much less do as well by their Roman Catholic brothers and sisters?

One of the most effective of all the concerted efforts in this country in teaching the art of Christian acquaintance has been that of the United Church Women (a general department in the Division of Christian Unity of the National Council of Churches). Their program moves across national, racial, and denominational lines, "seeking to unite the great body of Protestant and Orthodox women in service for God and his kingdom," and the secret of their success has been their constant stress on *local* ecumenism. Their sponsorship of the World Day of Prayer, May Fellowship Day, and World Community Day has provided for numberless women the vital stuff of ecumenical encounter.

Ecumenical study has three linked dimensions. The first is *comparative* study, in an interdenominational group, of various topics that touch on their own respective traditions or that concern some vital phase of the ecumenical movement. At the most elementary level, this would begin with what might be called "denominational profiles"—surveys of the history, distinctive witness, and ecumenical attitudes of the respective denominations represented.

Or, the group might choose to explore the current Consultation on Church Union as an important project affecting many of the mainline American churches. The "minutes" and "position papers" of the Consultation are available for first-hand examination and discussion.[4] Additional help would be available from any of the delegates

4 From Dr. George L. Hunt, Executive Secretary, Consultation on Church Union, Box 69, Fanwood, N.J. See "Books on Ecumenicity," p. 181.

of the member churches who may live nearby and from other local leaders of special competence.

A third profitable topic for comparative study would be those various reports and resolutions of the National Council of Churches or the World Council of Churches' conferences that were, as we have said, referred to the churches but still are waiting for "study and appropriate action," at least at the local level. For example, there is the New Delhi Statement on "Unity,"[5] or the Oberlin report on "The Table of the Lord,"[6] or the Montreal report on "Scripture and Tradition"[7] (to mention only three out of a dozen or more possibilities). Here, as with the Consultation on Church Union material, the logical steps in a study program would be: (1) review of the basic texts; (2) consultation with members of your denominational commission on ecumenical affairs[8] (or its equivalent); (3) help from available resource persons in your region.

Finally, there is also the rather obvious choice of a study program about the Second Vatican Council, especially if your group has Roman Catholic members or could bring them in. Here, the most immediately relevant topics would be the decree *On Ecumenism* or "On the Laity," which is Chapter Four of the constitution *On the Church*. The of-

---

[5] See below, Appendix VII, p. 165: *The New Delhi Report.*

[6] Paul S. Minear (ed.), *The Nature of the Unity We Seek*, pp. 199-205.

[7] P. C. Rodger and Lukas Vischer (eds.), *The Fourth World Conference on Faith and Order; Montreal, 1963* (New York: Association Press, 1964), pp. 50-61.

[8] General Commission on Ecumenical Affairs of The Methodist Church, 1200 Davis St., Evanston, Ill. 60201, Rev. Robert W. Huston, General Secretary [and the Committee on Ecumenical Relations, Woman's Division, Board of Missions of The Methodist Church, Room 1420, 475 Riverside Drive, New York, N.Y. 10027, Mrs. A. B. Pfeiffer, Chairman.]

ficial texts of these are available in inexpensive pamphlet form, and the Roman Catholic periodicals have been full of comments about them since their promulgation in 1964. It would be important of course for the Protestants to react as directly and candidly as possible—and for the Catholics to be asked to explain what these statements mean to them in the light of their own *pre*-Vatican experience and understanding.

There are some basic ground rules that should govern the course of all serious ecumenical study. In the very first session of the Vatican Council Bishop Emile De Smedt of Bruges, Belgium, laid these out in summary fashion for Catholics—but, with suitable adjustments, they can apply to us all:

(1) Understand the present-day teachings of the Orthodox and Protestant Churches [we *might add Roman*]. We must be well acquainted with their faith, their liturgical life, their theology.

(2) Know what opinion they have about our teaching, the points they understand correctly and the points they do not understand.

(3) Know what non-Catholics feel is missing or not sufficiently explained in Catholic doctrine—for example, the teaching of the Word of God, on the priesthood of the faithful, on religious liberty.

(4) Examine whether our manner of expression contains statements or ways of saying things difficult for non-Catholics [non-Methodists?] to understand. . . .

(5) Select our words, images, figures of speech with a regard to the reaction they are likely to produce in the minds and sensibilities of non-Catholics.

(6) Weigh our judgments and look at them in a context that will be acceptable to non-Catholics.

(7) Present our arguments (with citations and reasons) in a persuasive manner.

(8) Avoid any sterile polemics.

(9) Indicate errors in a way that is not offensive to the persons who are in error.[9]

It must not be forgotten that the results of meaningful study at the local level may also have an important feedback into the wider circles of the movement. Denominational commissions and the study departments of the National Council of Churches and the World Council of Churches are greatly interested in the work of local and regional study groups and use their reports in planning their own programs. The Oberlin Conference of 1957 was an outstanding example of this sort of cooperation. A local group might very well consider as a project the formulation of its experiences and conclusions in written form and forward these to the appropriate officials.[10] If we had a fairly large and representative collection of such reports, both the National Council of Churches and the World Council of Churches could proceed far more intelligently and realistically in their appraisal of our overall

[9] Robert Kaiser, *Pope, Council and World* (New York: The Macmillan Co., 1963), p. 178.

[10] Rev. Wm. A. Norgren, Department of Faith and Order, National Council of the Churches of Christ in the United States of America, 475 Riverside Drive, New York, N.Y. 10027.

Dr. Lukas Vischer, Department of Faith and Order, World Council of Churches, 150 route de Ferney, Geneva, Switzerland.

Miss Margaret Shannon, Executive Director, Department of United Church Women, Division of Christian Unity, National Council of the Churches of Christ in the U.S.A., Room 812, 475 Riverside Drive, New York, N.Y.

progress in ecumenical growth and tension.

Beyond this level of comparative study about ecumenical issues, as such, there is another which would greatly extend and deepen the ecumenical experience of the group. This would be a program of planned experiments in ecumenical *worship,* again, at the local level. One of the most interesting of these experiments would be with an exploration of the ecumenical treasures in our various hymnals and "books of worship." Not many church folk realize that these hymnals and prayer books are the most truly ecumenical documents in our churches, excepting only the Holy Scriptures. In all but the worst of them, there are hymns and hymn tunes from every age of the church's history, from every region in which it has been settled, from every tradition that has emerged over the years. With some study and ingenuity these various "types" can be sorted out and identified; and then played, sung, and discussed by the group. This has the added advantage of promoting the learning of some great hymns that may not have been familiar to all and of gaining new insights into our own "old standbys" that could come from those who would be coming at them afresh. Such a study would reveal the marvelous common heritage which we share with all Christians in the prayer life of the community across the ages and across our tragic rifts.

All this would, of course, be background for further experiments in joint services of *corporate worship*—the sharing of all in authentic *liturgy,* ordered according to the *rituals* of one or another of the churches to which we belong. Arranging for joint services such as in the Week of Prayer for Christian Unity is bound to be difficult in some cases and easy in others, depending on the local situation and the dispositions of the local clergy. This, at least, should be possible anywhere: the study group would be welcomed at each of its members' local churches for any stated service of public worship. Thereafter, it would be profitable to review impressions expressed by its members and their questions with the minister and the official board. Such visits could be planned to include various occasions (such as baptisms, weddings, and funerals)— and so nourish the spiritual lives of the participants even as they are helped to understand the realities and dilemmas of the ecumenical situation.

In the past, it would have been impossible for Roman Catholics to join with Protestants in such liturgical experiments. Happily, this is no longer the case. The decree *On Ecumenism* makes explicit provision for such experiments, and a "Directory" explaining the terms and limits of such "common worship" has been issued by the Secretariat for Promoting Christian Unity:

> In certain special circumstances such as in prayer services "for unity" and during ecumenical gatherings, it is allowable, indeed desirable, that Catholics should join in prayer with their separated brethren. Such prayers in common are certainly a very effective means of petitioning for the grace of unity and they are a genuine expression of the ties which still bind Catholics to their separated brethren. "For where two or three are gathered together in my name, there am I in the midst of them" (Matt. 18:20). . . .
>
> We must get to know the outlook of our separated brethren. Study is absolutely required for this and it should be pursued in fidelity to truth and with a spirit of good will. Catholics who already have a proper grounding need to

acquire a more adequate understanding of the respective doctrines of our separated brethren, their history, their spiritual and liturgical life, their religious psychology and cultural background.[11]

If ecumenical *study* and *worship* are to have their full effect, they must issue in some expression at still a third level, that of *ecumenism in action*. Here again the local situation must indicate what is needed, what is possible, and how best to make the venture. Nobody yet knows how many useful things there are for Christians to do together in any given locality. The only rule to remember is that it is poor ecumenism for any group to get into overlapping competition with some similar "ecumenical" venture.

Where are the *growing edges* of the church in *your* community? The "inner city"? The lost world of the apartment dwellers? The shifting social patterns in town and country? What are the *issues* that challenge all the churches most urgently? Civil rights? Juvenile delinquency? Labor-management relations? The creative use of leisure time? Mental health? Community concern for the lonely and the elderly? Would not concerted Christian action be more practically effective in dealing constructively with the above situations than any of the programs now planned or contemplated in the separate congregations? What can *all* of the churches in your community do *together* that would add strength and impact to what they are already doing separately? Can you think of various ways by which you could discover what, in your particular situation, has been regarded as fixed and yet

[11]Vatican II's *Decree On Ecumenism* (Rome: Typis Polyglottis Vaticanis, 1965), Chap. II, Sec. 8.

might turn out to be fluid? For example, in 1964 Bishop James K. Mathews (The Methodist Church) and Bishop Anson Phelps Stokes, Jr. (Protestant Episcopal Church) both of Boston—without consultation or the prior knowledge of either—appointed two ministers to organize new congregations in a growing suburb in their overlapping episcopal areas. After initial studies and discussion between themselves, the two men approached their bishops with the unconventional proposal that one church could be built to serve both Methodists and Episcopalians in that place, with a joint ministry. Moreover, the bishops were mildly startled to discover, upon examination, that none of the existing legislation in their two churches actually *forbids* such an arrangement, under certain conditions. Here again, as so often, the most urgent question is not what is permissible, but what is *possible*. But as *this* question keeps being raised by loyal churchmen, convinced that it is the church and her mission that stand to gain from positive answers, so then, with cumulative force, will the cause of Christian unity be fostered and forwarded— upborne by the groundswell of the communal experiences of Christians, "all in each place."

The most obvious value to come from similar patterns of "local ecumenism" would be a church membership well enough informed to understand and to react responsibly to the unfolding developments of the ecumenical movement around the world and in their respective denominations and councils and conferences. But there is another, and more potentially important, result that can be envisaged: an intelligent, responsible impatience on the part of church members regarding their denomination's participation and progress in the movement as a whole.

It is high time that our denominational leaders were made aware of a rising tide of loyal discontent and respectful criticism of the all too deliberate speed with which we seem to be shuffling toward our professed goals of Christian unity. Our leaders rightly explain that they can move no faster than the people will support them. Yet the sort of do-it-yourself ecumenism of which we have been speaking would generate that support where it really counts. And, there is considerable evidence that the laity, by and large, are more open to challenges and risks of unity than are some clergy. In any case, an informed and concerned laity, posing the right ecumenical questions in their churches, would supply much-needed motive power for the rough road ahead.

And yet for all our talk about ecumenical problems and possibilities, the heart of the matter lies elsewhere: in our life that is hid with God in Christ. Nothing will finally serve the cause of valid-unity-on-behalf-of-church-in-mission unless it is rooted in the vital source of that mission—*living faith*. Sections 7 and 8 of the Vatican II's *Decree On Ecumenism* declare:

> There can be no ecumenism worthy of the name without interior conversion. For it is from new attitudes of mind — from self-denial and unstinted love — that desires of unity take their rise and develop in a mature way. We should therefore pray to the Holy Spirit for the grace to be genuinely self-denying, humble, gentle in the service of others and to have an attitude of brotherly generosity towards them. . . .
>
> The faithful should remember that they are better promoting union among Christians — indeed living it better — the

more they strive to live holier lives according to the gospel. For the closer their union with the Father, the Word and the Spirit, the more deeply and easily will they be able to grow in mutual brotherly love.

This change of heart and holiness of life, along with public and private prayer for the unity of Christians should be regarded as the soul of the whole ecumenical movement, and it merits the name "spiritual ecumenism."

With suitable shifts of accent, the rest of us can surely say "Amen" to that.

Now, in perspective, we can see that the first half of this century was a time of thawing and planting and cultivation—the thawing of the bitter chill of "Christians" in estrangement and separation from one another; of the planting of the seeds of ecumenism in a soil warmed by an aroused sense of mission; of the cultivation of the fresh growth of Christian fellowship, community, and service. Epochal as these developments have been, they are only harbingers and omens of what yet may come to pass. The cause of Christian unity has not yet come to have top priority in our denominations nor is it a prime value for the majority of Christians in those churches. But the tide rises and the spread of intelligent interest in ecumenical affairs widens.

It does not exceed a devout imagination to suppose that the last half of this century may, in the providence of God, be the season of harvest—of the culmination of the labors and hopes of those who "died in [this] faith, not having received the promises, but having seen them afar off, and were persuaded of them, and embraced them, . . . and these all, having obtained a good report through faith, received not the promise: God having provided some better thing for us, that they without us should not be made perfect" (Heb. 11:13, 39-40, KJV). It cannot be beyond the possibilities of faith that God will give our children the fullness of what we can foretaste—if in this, our present, *we* dedicate ourselves to pray and work and hope for that unity which can be

> . . . made visible as all in each place, who are baptized into Jesus Christ and confess him as Lord and Savior, are brought by the Holy Spirit into one fully committed fellowship, holding the one apostolic faith, preaching the one Gospel, breaking the one bread, joining in common prayer, and having a corporate life reaching out in witness and service to all. . . .[12]

There is, of course, no guaranteeing that this will come to pass, or even a guarantee that our human history on this planet has that much of a future. But whatever the future, it will be the better if we have done all that love and self-forgetfulness can do to heal "the sixth wound of Christ"—his sundered body. Only in this way can we who call and profess ourselves Christian be truly obedient, in our own times and places, to the manifest petition of our Lord: that we love one another as we have been loved by God in Christ and give witness to that love in service to all our neighbors to the end that the world which Christ died to save may truly believe—and so be *saved!*

[12]See below, Appendix VII, p. 165: *The New Delhi Report.*

First World Conference on Faith and Order

*"The Church's Message to the World—
The Gospel!"*

The message of the Church to the world is and must always remain the Gospel of Jesus Christ. The Gospel is the joyful message of redemption, both here and hereafter, the gift of God to sinful man in Jesus Christ.

The world was prepared for the coming of Christ through the activities of God's Spirit in all humanity, but especially in His revelation as given in the Old Testament; and in the fulness of time the eternal Word of God became incarnate, and was made man, Jesus Christ, the Son of God and the Son of Man, full of grace and truth.

Through His life and teaching, His call to repentance, His proclamation of the coming of the Kingdom of God and of judgment, His suffering and death, His resurrection and exaltation to the right hand of the Father, and by the mission of the Holy Spirit, He has brought to us forgiveness of sins, and has revealed the fulness of the living God and His boundless love toward us. By the appeal of that love, shown in its completeness on the Cross, He summons us to the new life of faith, self-sacrifice, and devotion to His service and the service of men.

Jesus Christ, as the crucified and the living One, as

Saviour and Lord, is also the centre of the world-wide
Gospel of the Apostles and the Church. Because He Himself is the Gospel, the Gospel is the message of the Church
to the world. It is more than a philosophical theory; more
than a theological system; more than a programme for
material betterment. The Gospel is rather the gift of a new
world from God to this old world of sin and death; still
more, it is the victory over sin and death, the revelation
of eternal life in Him who has knit together the whole
family in heaven and on earth in the communion of saints,
united in the fellowship of service, of prayer, and of praise.

The Gospel is the prophetic call to sinful man to turn to
God, the joyful tidings of justification and of sanctification
to those who believe in Christ. It is the comfort of those
who suffer; to those who are bound it is the assurance of
the glorious liberty of the sons of God. The Gospel brings
peace and joy to the heart, and produces in men self-
denial, readiness for brotherly service, and compassionate
love. It offers the supreme goal for the aspirations of
youth, strength to the toiler, rest to the weary, and the
crown of life to the martyr.

The Gospel is the sure source of power for social re-
generation. It proclaims the only way by which humanity
can escape from those class and race hatreds which devas-
tate society at present into the enjoyment of national well-
being and international friendship and peace. It is also a
gracious invitation to the non-Christian world, East and
West, to enter into the joy of the living Lord.

Sympathizing with the anguish of our generation, with
its longing for intellectual sincerity, social justice and
spiritual inspiration, the Church in the eternal Gospel
meets the needs and fulfils the God-given aspirations of

the modern world. Consequently, as in the past so also in the present, the Gospel is the only way of salvation. Thus, through His Church, the living Christ still says to men "Come unto me! . . . He that followeth me shall not walk in darkness, but shall have the light of life."

[Lukas Vischer (ed.), *A Documentary History of the Faith and Order Movement 1927-63*. Copyright and used by permission of the World Council of Churches (St. Louis, Mo.: The Bethany Press, 1963), pp. 29-30.]

Pope Pius XI's Encyclical

"The Promotion of Authentic
Religious Unity"

VENERABLE BRETHREN:

HEALTH AND APOSTOLIC BENEDICTION!

Never perhaps in the past have the minds of men been so engrossed as they are today with the desire to strengthen and extend for the common good of mankind that tie of brotherhood—the result of our common origin and nature —which binds us all so closely together. The world does not yet fully enjoy the fruits of peace; on the contrary, dissensions old and new in various lands still issue in rebellions and conflict. Such disputes, affecting the tranquil prosperity of nations, can never be settled without the combined and active goodwill of those who are responsible for their government, and hence it is easy to understand— especially now that the unity of mankind is no longer called into question—the widespread desire that all nations, in view of this universal kinship, should daily find closer union with one another.

It is with a similar motive that efforts are being made by some, in connexion with the New Law promulgated by Christ our Lord. Assured that there exist few men who are entirely devoid of the religious sense, they seem to ground on this belief a hope that all nations, while differing indeed in religious matters, may yet without great difficulty be brought to fraternal agreement on certain points of doctrine which will form a common basis of the spiritual life. With this object congresses, meetings, and addresses are arranged, attended by a large concourse of hearers, where all without distinction, unbelievers of every kind as well as Christians, even those who unhappily have rejected Christ and denied His divine nature or mission, are invited to join in the discussion. Now, such efforts can meet with no kind of approval among Catholics. They presuppose the erroneous view that all religions are more or less good and praiseworthy, inasmuch as all give expression, under various forms, to that innate sense which leads men to God and to the obedient acknowledgment of His rule. Those who hold such a view are not only in error; they distort the true idea of religion, and thus reject it, falling gradually into naturalism and atheism. To favor this opinion, therefore, and to encourage such undertakings is tantamount to abandoning the religion revealed by God.

Nevertheless, when there is a question of fostering unity among Christians, it is easy for many to be misled by the apparent excellence of the object to be achieved. Is it not right, they ask, is it not the obvious duty of all who invoke the name of Christ to refrain from mutual reproaches and at last to be united in charity? Dare any one say that he loves Christ, and yet not strive with all his might to accomplish the desire of Him Who asked His Father that His disciples might be "one" (John 17:21[1])? Did not Christ will that mutual charity should be the distinguishing char-

---

[1] Douay and Confraternity versions are used in Vatican encyclicals and decrees.

acteristic of His disciples? "By this shall all men know that you are My disciples, if you have love one for another" (John 13:35). If only all Christians were "one," it is contended, then they might do so much more to drive out the pest of irreligion which with its insidious and far-reaching advance is threatening to sap the strength of the Gospel. These and similar arguments, with amplifications, are constantly on the lips of the "pan-Christians" who, so far from being a few isolated individuals, have formed an entire class and grouped themselves into societies of extensive membership, usually under the direction of non-Catholics, who also disagree in matters of faith. The energy with which this scheme is being promoted has won for it many adherents, and even many Catholics are attracted by it, since it holds out the hope of a union apparently consonant with the wishes of Holy Mother Church, whose chief desire it is to recall her erring children and to bring them back to her bosom. In reality, however, these fair and alluring words cloak a most grave error, subversive of the foundations of the Catholic faith.

Conscious, therefore, of Our Apostolic office, which warns Us not to allow the flock of Christ to be led astray by harmful fallacies, We invoke your zeal, Venerable Brethren, to avert this evil. We feel confident that each of you, by written and spoken word, will explain clearly to the people the principles and arguments that We are about to set forth, so that Catholics may know what view and what course of action they should adopt regarding schemes for the promiscuous union into one body of all who call themselves Christians.

God, the Creator of all things, made us that we might know Him and serve Him; to our service, therefore, He has a full right. He might indeed have been contented to prescribe for man's government the natural law alone, that is, the law which in creation He has written upon man's heart, and have regulated the progress of that law by His ordinary Providence. He willed, however, to make positive laws which we should obey, and progressively, from the beginnings of the human race until the coming and preaching of Jesus Christ, He Himself taught mankind the duties which a rational creature owes to his Creator. "God, Who at sundry times and in divers manners spoke in times past to the fathers by the prophets, last of all in these days hath spoken to us by His Son" (Heb. 1:1, seq.). Evidently, therefore, no religion can be true save that which rests upon the revelation of God, a revelation begun from the very first, continued under the Old Law, and brought to completion by Jesus Christ Himself under the New. Now, if God has spoken—and it is historically certain that He has in fact spoken—then it is clearly man's duty implicitly to believe His revelation and to obey His commands. That we might rightly do both, for the glory of God and for our own salvation, the only-begotten Son of God founded His Church on earth. None, we think, of those who claim to be Christians will deny that a Church, and one sole Church, was founded by Christ.

On the further question, however, as to what in the intention of its Founder was to be the precise nature of that Church, there is not the same agreement. Many of them, for example, deny that the Church of Christ was intended to be visible and manifest, at any rate in the sense that it was to be visibly the one body of the faithful, agreeing in one and the same doctrine under one teaching and governing authority. They conceive the visible Church as nothing more than a federation of the various Christian communities, even though these may hold different and mutually exclusive doctrines. The truth is that Christ founded His Church as a perfect society, of its nature external and perceptible to the senses, which in the future should carry on the work of the salvation of mankind under one head, with a living teaching authority, administering the sacraments which are the sources of heavenly grace (John 3:5; 6:48-59; 20-22 seq.; cf. Matt. 18:18, etc.). Wherefore He compared His Church to a kingdom (Matt. 13), to a house (cf. Matt. 16:18), to a sheepfold (John 10:16), and to a flock (John 21:15-17). The Church thus wondrously instituted could not cease to exist with the death of its Founder and of the Apostles, the pioneers of its propagation; for its mission was to lead all men to salvation, without distinction of time or place: "Going therefore, teach ye all nations" (Matt. 28:19). Nor could the Church ever lack the effective strength necessary for the continued accomplishment of its task, since Christ Himself is perpetually present with it, according to His promise: "Behold, I am with you all days, even to the consummation of the world" (Matt. 28:20). Hence not only must the Church still exist today and continue always to exist, but it must ever be exactly the same as it was in the days of the Apostles. Otherwise we must say— which God forbid—that Christ has failed in His purpose, or that He erred when He asserted of His Church that the gates of hell should never prevail against it (Matt. 16:18).

And here it will be opportune to expound and to reject a certain false opinion which lies at the root of this question and of that complex movement by which non-Catholics seek to bring about the union of Christian Churches.

Those who favor this view constantly quote the words of Christ, "That they may be one . . . And there shall be one fold, and one shepherd" (John 17:21, 10:16), in the sense that Christ thereby merely expressed a desire or a prayer which as yet has not been granted. For they hold that the unity of faith and government which is a note of the one true Church of Christ has up to the present time hardly ever existed, and does not exist today. They consider that this unity is indeed to be desired and may even, by co-operation and goodwill, be actually attained, but that meanwhile it must be regarded as a mere ideal. The Church, they say, is of its nature divided into sections, composed of several churches or distinct communities which still remain separate, and although holding in common some articles of doctrine, nevertheless differ concerning the remainder; that all these enjoy the same rights; and that the Church remained one and undivided at the most only from the Apostolic age until the first Oecumenical Councils. Hence, they say, controversies and long-standing differences, which today still keep asunder the members of the Christian family, must be entirely set aside, and from the residue of doctrines a common form of faith drawn up and proposed for belief, in the profession of which all may not only know but also feel themselves to be brethren. If the various Churches or communities were united in some kind of universal federation, they would then be in a position to oppose resolutely and successfully the progress of irreligion.

Such, Venerable Brethren, is the common contention. There are indeed some who recognize and affirm that Protestantism has with inconsiderate zeal rejected certain articles of faith and external ceremonies which are in fact useful and attractive, and which the Roman Church still retains. But they immediately go on to say that the Roman Church, too, has erred, and corrupted the primitive religion by adding to it and proposing for belief doctrines not only alien to the Gospel but contrary to its spirit. Chief among these they count that of the primacy of jurisdiction granted to Peter and to his successors in the See of Rome. There are actually some, though few, who grant to the Roman Pontiff a primacy of honour and even a certain power or jurisdiction; this, however, they consider to arise not from the divine law but merely from the consent of the faithful. Others, again, even go so far as to desire the Pontiff himself to preside over their mixed assemblies. For the rest, while you may hear many non-Catholics loudly preaching brotherly communion in Jesus Christ, yet not one will you find to whom it ever occurs with devout submission to obey the Vicar of Jesus Christ in his capacity of teacher or ruler. Meanwhile they assert their readiness to treat with the Church of Rome, but on equal terms, as equals with an equal. But even if they could so treat, there seems little doubt that they would do so only on condition that no pact into which they might enter should compel them to retract those opinions which still keep them outside the one fold of Christ.

This being so, it is clear that the Apostolic See can by no means take part in these assemblies, nor is it in any way lawful for Catholics to give to such enterprises their encouragement or support. If they did so, they would be giving countenance to a false Christianity quite alien to the one Church of Christ. Shall we commit the iniquity of suffering the truth, the truth revealed by God, to be made a subject for compromise? For it is indeed a question of defending revealed truth. Jesus Christ sent His Apostles into the whole world to declare the faith of the Gospel to every nation, and, to save them from error. He willed that the Holy Ghost should first teach them all truth. Has this doctrine, then, disappeared, or at any time been obscured, in the Church of which God Himself is the ruler and guardian? Our Redeemer plainly said that His Gospel was intended not only for the apostolic age but for all time. Can the object of faith, then, have become in the process of time so dim and uncertain that today we must tolerate contradictory opinions? If this were so, then we should have to admit that the coming of the Holy Ghost upon the Apostles, the perpetual indwelling of the same Spirit in the Church, nay, the very preaching of Jesus Christ, have centuries ago lost their efficacy and value. To affirm this would be blasphemy. The only-begotten Son of God not only bade His representatives to teach all nations; He also obliged all men to give credence to whatever was taught them by "witnesses preordained by God" (Acts 10:41). Moreover, He enforced His command with this sanction: "He that believeth and is baptized shall be saved; he that believeth not shall be condemned" (Mark 16:16). These two commands, the one to teach, the other to believe for salvation, must be obeyed. But they cannot even be understood unless the Church proposes an inviolate and clear teaching and in proposing it is immune from all danger of error. It is also false to say that, although the deposit of truth does indeed exist, yet it is to be found only with such laborious effort and after such lengthy study and discussion, that a man's life is hardly long enough for its discovery and attainment. This would be equivalent to saying that the most merciful God spoke through the prophets and through His only-begotten Son merely in order that some few men, and those advanced in years, might learn what He had revealed, and not in order to inculcate a doctrine of faith and morals by which man should be guided throughout the whole of his life.

These pan-Christians who strive for the union of the Churches would appear to pursue the noblest of ideals in promoting charity among all Christians. But how should charity tend to the detriment of faith? Every one knows that John himself, the Apostle of love, who seems in his Gospel to have revealed the secrets of the Sacred Heart of Jesus, and who never ceased to impress upon the memory of his disciples the new commandment "to love one another," nevertheless strictly forbade any intercourse with those who professed a mutilated and corrupt form of Christ's teaching: "If any man come to you, and bring not this doctrine, receive him not into the house, nor say to him, God speed you" (II John 10).

Therefore, since the foundation of charity is faith pure and inviolate, it is chiefly by the bond of one faith that the disciples of Christ are to be united. A federation of Christians, then, is inconceivable in which each member retains his own opinions and private judgment in matters of faith, even though they differ from the opinions of all the rest. How can men with opposite convictions belong to one and the same federation of the faithful: those who accept sacred Tradition as a source of revelation and those who reject it; those who recognize as divinely constituted the hierarchy of bishops, priests, and ministers in the Church, and those who regard it as gradually introduced to suit the conditions of the time; those who adore Christ really present in the Most Holy Eucharist through that wonderful conversion of the bread and wine, transubstantiation, and those who assert that the body of Christ is there only by faith or by the signification and virtue of the sacrament; those who in the Eucharist recognize both sacrament and sacrifice, and those who say that it is nothing more than the memorial of the Lord's supper; those who think it right and useful to pray to the Saints reigning with Christ, especially to Mary the Mother of God, and to venerate their images, and those who refuse such veneration as derogatory to the honour due to Jesus Christ, "the one mediator of God and Men" (cf. I Tim. 2:5)?

How so great a variety of opinions can clear the way for the unity of the Church, We know not. That unity can arise only from one teaching authority, one law of belief, and one faith of Christians. But we do know that from such a state of affairs it is but an easy step to the neglect of religion or "indifferentism," and to the error of the modernists, who hold that dogmatic truth is not absolute but relative, that is, that it changes according to the varying necessities of time and place and the varying tendencies of the mind; that it is not contained in an immutable tradition, but can be altered to suit the needs of human life.

Furthermore, it is never lawful to employ in connexion with articles of faith the distinction invented by some between "fundamental" and "non-fundamental" articles, the former to be accepted by all, the latter being left to the free acceptance of the faithful. The supernatural virtue of faith has as its formal motive the authority of God revealing, and this allows of no such distinction. All true followers of Christ, therefore, will believe the dogma of the Immaculate Conception of the Mother of God with the same faith as they believe the mystery of the august Trin-

ity, the infallibility of the Roman Pontiff in the sense
defined by the Oecumenical Vatican Council with the
same faith as they believe the Incarnation of Our Lord.
That these truths have been solemnly sanctioned and defined by the Church at various times, some of them even
quite recently, makes no difference to their certainty, nor
to our obligation of believing them. Has not God revealed
them all?

The teaching authority of the Church in the divine wisdom was constituted on earth in order that the revealed
doctrines might remain for ever intact and might be
brought with ease and security to the knowledge of men.
This authority is indeed daily exercised through the Roman
Pontiff and the Bishops who are in communion with him;
but it has the further office of defining some truth with
solemn decree whenever it is opportune, and whenever
this is necessary either to oppose the errors or the attacks
of heretics, or again to impress the minds of the faithful
with a clearer and more detailed explanation of the articles
of sacred doctrine. But in the use of this extraordinary
teaching authority no fresh invention is introduced, nothing new is ever added to the number of those truths which
are at least implicitly contained within the deposit of
Revelation divinely committed to the Church; but truths
which to some perhaps may still seem obscure are rendered
clear, or a truth which some may have called into question
is declared to be of faith.

Thus, Venerable Brethren, it is clear why this Apostolic
See has never allowed its subjects to take part in the
assemblies of non-Catholics. There is but one way in
which the unity of Christians may be fostered, and that
is by furthering the return to the one true Church of

Christ of those who are separated from it; for from that one true Church they have in the past fallen away. The one Church of Christ is visible to all, and will remain, according to the will of its Author, exactly the same as He instituted it. The mystical Spouse of Christ has never in the course of centuries been contaminated, nor in the future can she ever be, as Cyprian bears witness: "The Bride of Christ cannot become false to her Spouse; she is inviolate and pure. She knows but one dwelling, and chastely and modestly she guards the sanctity of the nuptial chamber" (*De Cath. Ecclesiae unitate,* 6). The same holy martyr marvelled that any one could believe that "this unity of the Church built upon a divine foundation, knit together by heavenly sacraments, could ever be rent asunder by the conflict of wills" (*ibid.*). For since the mystical body of Christ, like His physical body, is one (I Cor. 12:12), compactly and fitly joined together (Eph. 4:16), it were foolish to say that the mystical body is composed of disjointed and scattered members. Whosoever therefore is not united with the body is no member thereof, neither is he in communion with Christ its head.

Furthermore, in this one Church of Christ no man can be or remain who does not accept, recognize, and obey the authority and supremacy of Peter and his legitimate successors. Did not the ancestors of those who are now entangled in the errors of Photius and of the Reformers obey the Bishop of Rome, the chief shepherd of souls? Their children, alas! have left the home of their fathers; but that house did not therefore fall to the ground and perish for ever, for it was supported by God. Let them, then, return to their Father, Who, forgetting the insults in the past heaped upon the Apostolic See, will accord them a most loving welcome. If, as they constantly say, they long to be united with Us and Ours, why do they not hasten to enter the Church, "the mother and mistress of all Christ's faithful"? (*Conc. Lateran*, 4, c. 5). Let them heed the words of Lactantius: "The Catholic Church is alone in keeping the true worship. This is the fount of truth, this is the house of faith, this the temple of God: if any man enter not here, or if any man go forth from it, he is a stranger to the hope of life and salvation. Let none delude himself with obstinate wrangling. For life and salvation are here concerned, and these will be lost for ever unless their interests be carefully and assiduously kept in mind" (*Divin. Inst.* 4:30, ii-12).

Let our separated children, therefore, draw nigh to the Apostolic See, set up in the City which Peter and Paul, Princes of the Apostles, consecrated by their blood; to the See which is "the root and womb whence issues the Church of God" (Cypr. *Ep.* 48 *ad Cornelium,* 3); and let them come, not with any intention or hope that "the Church of the living God, the pillar and ground of the truth" (I Tim. 3:15) will cast aside the integrity of the faith and tolerate their errors, but to submit themselves to its teaching and government. Would that the happy lot, denied to so many of Our Predecessors, might at last be Ours, to embrace with fatherly affection those children whose unhappy separation from Us We now deplore. Would that God our Saviour, "Who will have all men to be saved, and to come to the knowledge of the truth" (I Tim. 2:4), might hear our humble prayer and vouch-safe to recall to the unity of the Church all that are gone astray. To this all-important end We implore, and We desire that others should implore, the intercession of the

Blessed Virgin Mary, Mother of divine grace, Help of Christians, victorious over all heresies, that she may entreat for Us the speedy coming of that longed-for day, when all men shall hear the voice of her divine Son, and shall be "careful to keep the unity of the Spirit in the bond of peace" (Eph. 4:3).

You, Venerable Brethren, know how dear to Our heart is this desire, and We wish that our children also should know, not only those belonging to the Catholic fold, but also those separated from Us. If these will humbly beg light from heaven, there is no doubt but that they will recognize the one true Church of Jesus Christ, and entering therein, will at last be united with Us in perfect charity. In the hope of this fulfilment, and as a pledge of our fatherly goodwill, We impart most lovingly to you, Venerable Brethren, and to your clergy and people, the Apostolic Benediction.

Given at S. Peter's, Rome, on the 6th day of January, the Feast of the Epiphany of our Lord Jesus Christ, in the year 1928, the sixth of Our Pontificate.

Pius PP. XI.

[*Acta Apostolicae Sedis; Commentarium Officiale* (Romae: Typis Polyglottis Vaticanis, 1928), XX, pp. 5-16. Cf. G. K. A. Bell (ed.), *Documents on Christian Unity, A Selection from the First and Second Series, 1920-30* (London: Oxford University Press, 1955), pp. 188-200. Encyclical Letter (*Mortalium Animos*) of His Holiness, Pope Pius XI (Washington, D.C.: National Catholic Welfare Conference, 1928).]

International Missionary Council

"The Christian Message"

Our message is Jesus Christ. He is the revelation of what God is and of what man through Him may become. In Him we come face to face with the ultimate reality of the universe; He makes known to us God as our Father, perfect and infinite in love and in righteousness; for in Him we find God incarnate, the final, yet ever-unfolding, revelation of the God in whom we live and move and have our being.

We hold that through all that happens, in light and in darkness, God is working, ruling and overruling. Jesus Christ, in His life and through His death and resurrection, has disclosed to us the Father, the Supreme Reality, as almighty Love, reconciling the world to Himself by the Cross, suffering with men in their struggle against sin and evil, bearing with them and for them the burden of sin, forgiving them as they, with forgiveness in their own hearts, turn to Him in repentance and faith, and creating humanity anew for an ever-growing, ever-enlarging, ever-lasting life.

The vision of God in Christ brings and deepens the sense of sin and guilt. We are not worthy of His love; we have by our own fault opposed His holy will. Yet that same vision which brings the sense of guilt brings also the assurance of pardon, if only we yield ourselves in faith to the spirit of Christ so that His redeeming love may avail to reconcile us to God.

We reaffirm that God, as Jesus Christ has revealed Him, requires all His children, in all circumstances, at all times, and in all human relationships, to live in love and righteousness for His glory. By the resurrection of Christ and the gift of the Holy Spirit God offers His own power to men that they may be fellow workers with Him, and urges them on to a life of adventure and self-sacrifice in preparation for the coming of His Kingdom in its fulness.

THE MISSIONARY MOTIVE

If such is our message, the motive for its delivery should be plain. The Gospel is the answer to the world's greatest need. It is not our discovery or achievement; it rests on what we recognize as an act of God. It is first and foremost "Good News." It announces glorious Truth. Its very nature forbids us to say that it may be the right belief for some but not for others. Either it is true for all, or it is not true at all.

But questions concerning the missionary motive have been widely raised, and such a change in the habits of men's thoughts as the last generation has witnessed must call for a re-examination of these questions.

Accordingly we would lay bare the motives that impel us to the missionary enterprise. We recognize that the health of our movement and of our souls demands a self-criticism that is relentless and exacting.

In searching for the motives that impel us we find ourselves eliminating decisively and at once certain motives that may seem, in the minds of some, to have become

mixed up with purer motives in the history of the movement. We repudiate any attempt on the part of trade or of
governments, openly or covertly, to use the missionary
cause for ulterior purposes. Our Gospel by its very nature
and by its declaration of the sacredness of human personality stands against all exploitation of man by man, so that
we cannot tolerate any desire, conscious or unconscious,
to use this movement for purposes of fastening a bondage,
economic, political, or social, on any people.

Going deeper, on our part we would repudiate any
symptoms of a religious imperialism that would desire to
impose beliefs and practices on others in order to manage
their souls in their supposed interests. We obey a God
who respects our wills and we desire to respect those of
others.

Nor have we the desire to bind up our Gospel with
fixed ecclesiastical forms which derive their meaning from
the experience of the Western Church. Rather the aim
should be to place at the disposal of the younger churches
of all lands our collective and historic experience. We believe that much of that heritage has come out of reality
and will be worth sharing. But we ardently desire that the
younger churches should express the Gospel through their
own genius and through forms suitable to their racial heritage. There must be no desire to lord it over the personal
or collective faith of others.

Our true and compelling motive lies in the very nature
of the God to whom we have given our hearts. Since He is
love, His very nature is to share. Christ is the expression
in time of the eternal self-giving of the Father. Coming
into fellowship with Christ we find in ourselves an over-
mastering impulse to share Him with others. We are con-

strained by the love of Christ and by obedience to His last command. He Himself said, "I am come that they might have life, and that they might have it more abundantly," and our experience corroborates it. He has become life to us. We would share that life.

We are assured that Christ comes with an offer of life to man and to societies and to nations. We believe that in Him the shackles of moral evil and guilt are broken from human personality and that men are made free, and that such personal freedom lies at the basis of the freeing of society from cramping custom and blighting social practices and political bondage, so that in Christ men and societies and nations may stand up free and complete.

We find in Christ, and especially in His cross and resurrection, an inexhaustible source of power that makes us hope when there is no hope. We believe that through it men and societies and nations that have lost their moral nerve to live will be quickened into life.

We have a pattern in our minds as to what form that life should take. We believe in a Christlike world. We know nothing better; we can be content with nothing less. We do not go to the nations called non-Christian, because they are the worst of the world and they alone are in need —we go because they are a part of the world and share with us in the same human need—the need of redemption from ourselves and from sin, the need to have life complete and abundant and to be remade after this pattern of Christlikeness. We desire a world in which Christ will not be crucified but where His Spirit shall reign.

We believe that men are made for Christ and cannot really live apart from Him. Our fathers were impressed with the horror that men should die without Christ—we share that horror; we are impressed also with the horror that men should live without Christ.

Herein lies the Christian motive; it is simple. We cannot live without Christ and we cannot bear to think of men living without Him. We cannot be content to live in a world that is un-Christlike. We cannot be idle while the yearning of His heart for His brethren is unsatisfied.

Since Christ is the motive, the end of Christian missions fits in with that motive. Its end is nothing less than the production of Christlike character in individuals and societies and nations through faith in and fellowship with Christ the living Saviour, and through corporate sharing of life in a divine society.

Christ is our motive and Christ is our end. We must give nothing less, and we can give nothing more.

[*The World Mission of Christianity; Messages and Recommendations of the Enlarged Meeting of the International Missionary Council held at Jerusalem, March 24-April 8, 1928* (New York: Board of Foreign Missions of the Methodist Episcopal Church, International Missionary Council, 1928), pp. 7-11.]

Second World Conference on Faith and Order

"The Grace of Our Lord Jesus Christ"

With deep thankfulness to God for the spirit of unity, which by His gracious blessing upon us has guided and controlled all our discussions on this subject, we agree on the following statement and recognize that there is in connection with this subject no ground for maintaining-division between Churches.

(*i*) *The Meaning of Grace*

When we speak of God's grace, we think of God Himself as revealed in His Son Jesus Christ. The meaning of divine grace is truly known only to those who know that God is Love, and that all that He does is done in love in fulfilment of His righteous purposes. His grace is manifested in our creation, preservation, and all the blessings of this life, but above all in our redemption through the life, death, and resurrection of Jesus Christ, in the sending of the holy and life-giving Spirit, in the fellowship of the Church and in the gift of the Word and Sacraments.

Man's salvation and welfare have their source in God alone, who is moved to His gracious activity towards man not by any merit on man's part, but solely by His free, outgoing love.

(ii) Justification and Sanctification

God in His free outgoing love justifies and sanctifies us through Christ, and His grace thus manifested is appropriated by faith, which itself is the gift of God.

Justification and Sanctification are two inseparable aspects of God's gracious action in dealing with sinful man.

Justification is the act of God, whereby He forgives our sins and brings us into fellowship with Himself, who in Jesus Christ, and by His death upon the Cross, has condemned sin and manifested His love to sinners, reconciling the world to Himself.

Sanctification is the work of God, whereby through the Holy Spirit He continually renews us and the whole Church, delivering us from the power of sin, giving us increase in holiness, and transforming us into the likeness of His Son through participation in His death and in His risen life. This renewal, inspiring us to continual spiritual activity and conflict with evil, remains throughout the gift of God. Whatever our growth in holiness may be, our fellowship with God is always based upon God's forgiving grace.

Faith is more than intellectual acceptance of the revelation in Jesus Christ; it is wholehearted trust in God and His promises, and committal of ourselves to Jesus Christ as Saviour and Lord.

(iii) The Sovereignty of God and Man's Response

In regard to the relation of God's grace and man's freedom, we all agree simply upon the basis of Holy Scripture and Christian experience that the sovereignty of God is supreme. By the sovereignty of God we mean His all-controlling, all-embracing will and purpose revealed in Jesus Christ for each man and for all mankind. And we wish further to insist that this eternal purpose is the expression of God's own loving and holy nature. Thus we men owe our whole salvation to His gracious will. But, on the other hand, it is the will of God that His grace should be actively appropriated by man's own will and that for such decision man should remain responsible.

Many theologians have made attempts on philosophical lines to reconcile the apparent antithesis of God's sovereignty and man's responsibility, but such theories are not part of the Christian Faith.

We are glad to report that in this difficult matter we have been able to speak with a united voice, so that we have found that here there ought to be no ground for maintaining any division between Churches.

(iv) The Church and Grace

We agree that the Church is the Body of Christ and the blessed company of all faithful people, whether in heaven or on earth, the communion of saints. It is at once the realization of God's gracious purposes in creation and redemption, and the continuous organ of God's grace in Christ by the Holy Spirit, who is its pervading life, and who is constantly hallowing all its parts.

It is the function of the Church to glorify God in its life and worship, to proclaim the gospel to every creature, and to build up in the fellowship and life of the Spirit all believing people, of every race and nation. To this end God bestows His Grace in the Church on its members through His Word and Sacraments, and in the abiding presence of the Holy Spirit.

(v) *Grace, the Word and the Sacraments*

We agree that the Word and the Sacraments are gifts of God to the Church through Jesus Christ for the salvation of mankind. In both the grace of God in Christ is shown forth, given, and through faith received; and this grace is one and indivisible.

The Word is the appointed means by which God's grace is made known to men, calling them to repentence, assuring them of forgiveness, drawing them to obedience and building them up in the fellowship of faith and love.

The Sacraments are not to be considered merely in themselves, but always as sacraments of the Church, which is the Body of Christ. They have their significance in the continual working of the Holy Spirit, who is the life of the Church. Through the sacraments God develops in all its members a life of perpetual communion lived within its fellowship, and thus enables them to embody His will in the life of the world; but the loving-kindness of God is not to be conceived as limited by His sacraments.

Among or within the Churches represented by us there is a certain difference of emphasis placed upon the Word and the sacraments, but we agree that such a difference need not be a barrier to union.

(vi) *Sola Gratia*

Some Churches set great value on the expression *sola gratia,* while others avoid it. The phrase has been the subject of much controversy, but we can all join in the following statement: Our salvation is the gift of God and the fruit of His grace. It is not based on the merit of man, but has its root and foundation in the forgiveness which God in His grace grants to the sinner whom He receives to sanctify him. We do not, however, hold that the action of the divine grace overrides human freedom and responsibility; rather, it is only as response is made by faith to divine grace that true freedom is achieved. Resistance to the appeal of God's outgoing love spells, not freedom, but bondage, and perfect freedom is found only in complete conformity with the good and acceptable and perfect will of God.

[Lukas Vischer, *A Documentary History of the Faith and Order Movement, 1927-1963*. Copyright and used by permission of the World Council of Churches. Pp. 40-43. See also Leonard Hodgson (ed.), *The Second World Conference on Faith & Order* held at Edinburgh, August 3-18, 1937 (New York: The Macmillan Co., 1938), pp. 224-27.]

A Policy Statement
of the Central Committee,
World Council of Churches

*"The Church, The Churches
and the World Council of Churches"*

I. INTRODUCTION

The first Assembly at Amsterdam adopted a resolution on "the authority of the Council" which read:

"The World Council of Churches is composed of Churches which acknowledge Jesus Christ as God and Saviour. They find their unity in Him. They do not have to create their unity; it is the gift of God. But they know that it is their duty to make common cause in the search for the expression of that unity in work and in life. The Council desires to serve the Churches which are its constituent members as an instrument whereby they may bear witness together to their common allegiance to Jesus Christ, and cooperate in matters requiring united action. But the Council is far from desiring to usurp any of the functions which already belong to its constituent Churches, or to control them, or to legislate for them, and indeed is prevented by its constitution from doing so. Moreover, while earnestly seeking fellowship in thought and action for all its members, the Council disavows any thought of becoming a single unified church structure independent of the Churches which have joined in constituting the Council, or a structure dominated by a centralised administrative authority.

"The purpose of the Council is to express its unity in another way. Unity arises out of the love of God in Jesus Christ, which, binding the constituent Churches to Him, binds them to one another. It is the earnest desire of the Council that the Churches may be bound closer to Christ and therefore closer to one another. In the bond of His love, they will desire continually to pray for one another and to strengthen one another, in worship and in witness, bearing one another's burdens and so fulfilling the law of Christ."[1]

This statement authoritatively answered some of the questions which had arisen about the nature of the Council. But it is clear that other questions are now arising and some attempt to answer them must be made, especially in the face of a number of false or inadequate conceptions of the Council which are being presented.

II. THE NEED FOR FURTHER STATEMENT

The World Council of Churches represents a new and unprecedented approach to the problem of inter-Church relationships. Its purpose and nature can be easily misunderstood. So it is salutary that we should state more clearly and definitely what the World Council is and what it is not.

This more precise definition involves certain difficulties. It is not for nothing that the Churches themselves have refrained from giving detailed and precise definitions of the nature of the Church. If this is true of them, it is not to

[1] Amsterdam, Report of Committee II (Policy). Cf. Official Report, ed. by W. A. Visser't Hooft, p. 127.

be expected that the World Council can easily achieve a
definition which has to take account of all the various
ecclesiologies of its member Churches. The World Council
deals in a provisional way with divisions between existing
Churches, which ought not to be, because they contradict
the very nature of the Church. A situation such as this
cannot be met in terms of well-established precedents.
The main problem is how one can formulate the ecclesiological implications of a body in which so many different
conceptions of the Church are represented, without using
the categories or language of one particular conception of
the Church.

In order to clarify the notion of the World Council of
Churches it will be best to begin by a series of negations
so as to do away at the outset with certain misunderstandings which may easily arise or have already arisen, because
of the newness and unprecedented character of the underlying conception.

III. WHAT THE WORLD COUNCIL OF CHURCHES IS NOT

(1) *The World Council of Churches is not and must
never become a Super-Church.*

It is not a Super-Church. It is not the World Church.
It is not the *Una Sancta* of which the Creeds speak. This
misunderstanding arises again and again although it has
been denied as clearly as possible in official pronouncements of the Council. It is based on complete ignorance
of the real situation within the Council. For if the Council should in any way violate its own constitutional principle, that it cannot legislate or act for its member

Churches, it would cease to maintain the support of its membership.

In speaking of "member Churches," we repeat a phrase from the Constitution of the World Council of Churches; but membership in the Council does not in any sense mean that the Churches belong to a body which can take decisions for them. Each Church retains the constitutional right to ratify or to reject utterances or actions of the Council. The "authority" of the Council consists only "in the weight it carries with the Churches by its own wisdom" (William Temple).

> (2) *The purpose of the World Council of Churches is not to negotiate unions between Churches, which can only be done by the Churches themselves acting on their own initiative, but to bring the Churches into living contact with each other and to promote the study and discussion of the issues of Church unity.*

By its very existence and its activities the Council bears witness to the necessity of a clear manifestation of the oneness of the Church of Christ. But it remains the right and duty of each Church to draw from its ecumenical experience such consequences as it feels bound to do on the basis of its own convictions. No Church, therefore, need fear that the Council will press it into decisions concerning union with other Churches.

> (3) *The World Council cannot and should not be based on any one particular conception of the Church. It does not prejudge the ecclesiological problem.*

It is often suggested that the dominating or underlying conception of the Council is that of such and such a Church or such and such a school of theology. It may well be that at a certain particular conference or in a particular utterance one can find traces of the strong influence of a certain tradition or theology.

The Council as such cannot possibly become the instrument of one confession or school without losing its very *raison d'être*. There are room and space in the World Council for the ecclesiology of every Church which is ready to participate in the ecumenical conversation and which takes its stand on the Basis of the Council, which is "a fellowship of Churches which accept our Lord Jesus Christ as God and Saviour."

The World Council exists in order that different Churches may face their differences, and therefore no Church is obliged to change its ecclesiology as a consequence of membership in the World Council.

(4) *Membership in the World Council of Churches does not imply that a Church treats its own conception of the Church as merely relative.*

There are critics, and not infrequently friends, of the ecumenical movement who criticize or praise it for its alleged inherent latitudinarianism. According to them the ecumenical movement stands for the fundamental equality of all Christian doctrines and conceptions of the Church and is, therefore, not concerned with the question of truth. This misunderstanding is due to the fact that ecumenism has in the minds of these persons become identified with certain particular theories about unity, which have indeed played a role in ecumenical history, but which do not represent the common view of the movement as a whole, and have never been officially endorsed by the World Council.

(5) *Membership in the World Council does not imply the acceptance of a specific doctrine concerning the nature of Church unity.*

The Council stands for Church unity. But in its midst there are those who conceive unity wholly or largely as a full consensus in the realm of doctrine, others who conceive of it primarily as sacramental communion based on common church order, others who consider both indispensable, others who would only require unity in certain fundamentals of faith and order, again others who conceive the one Church exclusively as a universal spiritual fellowship, or hold that visible unity is inessential or even undesirable. But none of these conceptions can be called the ecumenical theory. The whole point of the ecumenical conversation is precisely that all these conceptions enter into dynamic relations with each other.

In particular, membership in the World Council does not imply acceptance or rejection of the doctrine that the unity of the Church consists in the unity of the invisible Church. Thus the statement in the Encyclical *Mystici Corporis* concerning what it considers the error of a spiritualized conception of unity does not apply to the World Council. The World Council does not "imagine a Church which one cannot see or touch, which would be only spiritual, in which numerous Christian bodies, though divided in matters of faith, would nevertheless be united through an invisible link." It does, however, include Churches which believe that the Church is essentially invisible as well as those which hold that visible unity is essential.

IV. THE ASSUMPTIONS UNDERLYING THE
WORLD COUNCIL OF CHURCHES

We must now try to define the positive assumptions which underlie the World Council of Churches and the ecclesiological implications of membership in it.

(1) *The member Churches of the Council believe that conversation, cooperation, and common witness of the Churches must be based on the common recognition that Christ is the Divine Head of the Body.*

The Basis of the World Council is the acknowledgment of the central fact that "other foundation can no man lay than that is laid, even Jesus Christ." It is the expression of the conviction that the Lord of the Church is God-among-us Who continues to gather His children and to build His Church Himself.

Therefore, no relationship between the Churches can have any substance or promise unless it starts with the common submission of the Churches to the Headship of Jesus Christ in His Church. From different points of view Churches ask, "How can men with opposite convictions belong to one and the same federation of the faithful?" A clear answer to that question was given by the Orthodox delegates in Edinburgh 1937 when they said: "In spite of all our differences, our common Master and Lord is *one*—Jesus Christ who will lead us to a more and more

close collaboration for the edifying of the Body of Christ."[2]
The fact of Christ's Headship over His people compels all
those who acknowledge Him to enter into real and close
relationships with each other—even though they differ in
many important points.

(2) *The member Churches of the World Council believe on the basis of the New Testament that the
Church of Christ is one.*

The ecumenical movement owes its existence to the fact
that this article of the faith has again come home to men
and women in many Churches with an inescapable force.
As they face the discrepancy between the truth that there
is and can be only one Church of Christ, and the fact that
there exist so many Churches which claim to be Churches
of Christ but are not in living unity with each other, they
feel a holy dissatisfaction with the present situation. The
Churches realize that it is a matter of simple Christian duty
for each Church to do its utmost for the manifestation of
the Church in its oneness, and to work and pray that
Christ's purpose for His Church should be fulfilled.

(3) *The member Churches recognize that the membership of the Church of Christ is more inclusive than
the membership of their own Church body. They
seek, therefore, to enter into living contact with
those outside their own ranks who confess the
Lordship of Christ.*

2 From the statement presented to the Conference by Archbishop Germanos
on behalf of the Orthodox delegates. The statement is not part of the
conference report. It is printed in the minutes. Cf. Official Report, ed.
by L. Hodgson, p. 157.

All the Christian Churches, including the Church of Rome, hold that there is no complete identity between the membership of the Church Universal and the membership of their own Church. They recognize that there are Church members *extra muros,* that these belong *aliquo modo* to the Church, or even that there is an *ecclesia extra ecclesiam.* This recognition finds expression in the fact that with very few exceptions the Christian Churches accept the baptism administered by other Churches as valid.

But the question arises what consequences are to be drawn from this teaching. Most often in Church history the Churches have only drawn the negative consequence that they should have no dealings with those outside their membership. The underlying assumption of the ecumenical movement is that each Church has a positive task to fulfil in this realm. That task is to seek fellowship with all those who, while not members of the same visible body, belong together as members of the mystical body. And the ecumenical movement is the place where this search and discovery take place.

(4) *The member Churches of the World Council consider the relationship of other Churches to the Holy Catholic Church which the Creeds profess as a subject for mutual consideration. Nevertheless, membership does not imply that each Church must regard the other member Churches as Churches in the true and full sense of the word.*

There is a place in the World Council both for those Churches which recognize other Churches as Churches in the full and true sense, and for those who do not. But these divided Churches, even if they cannot yet accept each other as true and pure Churches, believe that they should not remain in isolation from each other, and consequently they have associated themselves in the World Council of Churches.

They know that differences of faith and order exist, but they recognize one another as serving the One Lord, and they wish to explore their differences in mutual respect, trusting that they may thus be led by the Holy Spirit to manifest their unity in Christ.

(5) *The member Churches of the World Council recognize in other Churches elements of the true Church. They consider that this mutual recognition obliges them to enter into a serious conversation with each other in the hope that these elements of truth will lead to the recognition of the full truth and to unity based on the full truth.*

It is generally taught in the different Churches that other Churches have certain elements of the true Church, in some traditions called *vestigia ecclesiae*. Such elements are the preaching of the Word, the teaching of the Holy Scriptures, and the administration of the sacraments. These elements are more than pale shadows of the life of the true Church. They are a fact of real promise and provide an opportunity to strive by frank and brotherly intercourse for the realization of a fuller unity. Moreover, Christians of all ecclesiological views throughout the world, by the preaching of the Gospel, brought men and women to salvation by Christ, to newness of life in Him, and into Christian fellowship with one another.

The ecumenical movement is based upon the conviction that these "traces" are to be followed. The Churches should not despise them as mere elements of truth but rejoice in them as hopeful signs pointing toward real unity. For what are these elements? Not dead remnants of the past but powerful means by which God works. Questions may and must be raised about the validity and purity of teaching and sacramental life, but there can be no question that such dynamic elements of Church life justify the hope that the Churches which maintain them will be led into fuller truth. It is through the ecumenical conversation that this recognition of truth is facilitated.

(6) *The member Churches of the Council are willing to consult together in seeking to learn of the Lord Jesus Christ what witness He would have them to bear to the world in His Name.*

Since the very *raison d'être* of the Church is to witness to Christ, Churches cannot meet together without seeking from their common Lord a common witness before the world. This will not always be possible. But when it proves possible thus to speak or act together, the Churches can gratefully accept it as God's gracious gift that in spite of their disunity He has enabled them to render one and the same witness and that they may thus manifest something of the unity, the purpose of which is precisely "that the world may believe," and that they may "testify that the Father has sent the Son to be the Saviour of the world."

(7) *A further practical implication of common membership in the World Council is that the member*

Churches should recognize their solidarity with each other, render assistance to each other in case of need, and refrain from such actions as are incompatible with brotherly relationships.

Within the Council the Churches seek to deal with each other with a brotherly concern. This does not exclude extremely frank speaking to each other, in which within the Council the Churches ask each other searching questions and face their differences. But this is to be done for the building up the Body of Christ. This excludes a purely negative attitude of one Church to another. The positive affirmation of each Church's faith is to be welcomed, but actions incompatible with brotherly relationships towards other member Churches defeat the very purpose for which the Council has been created. On the contrary, these Churches should help each other in removing all obstacles to the free exercise of the Church's normal functions. And whenever a Church is in need or under persecution, it should be able to count on the help of the other Churches through the Council.

(8) *The member Churches enter into spiritual relationships through which they seek to learn from each other and to give help to each other in order that the Body of Christ may be built up and that the life of the Churches may be renewed.*

It is the common teaching of the Churches that the Church as the temple of God is at the same time a building which has been built and a building which is being built. The Church has, therefore, aspects which belong to its very structure and essence and cannot be changed. But it has other aspects, which are subject to change. Thus the life of the Church, as it expresses itself in its witness to its own members and to the world, needs constant renewal. The Churches can and should help each other in this realm by a mutual exchange of thought and of experience. This is the significance of the study-work of the World Council and of many other of its activities. There is no intention to impose any particular pattern of thought or life upon the Churches. But whatever insight has been received by one or more Churches is to be made available to all the Churches for the sake of the "building up of the Body of Christ."

None of these positive assumptions, implied in the existence of the World Council, is in conflict with the teachings of the member Churches. We believe therefore that no Church need fear that by entering into the World Council it is in danger of denying its heritage.

As the conversation between the Churches develops and as the Churches enter into closer contact with each other, they will no doubt have to face new decisions and problems. For the Council exists to break the deadlock between the Churches. But in no case can or will any Church be pressed to take a decision against its own conviction or desire. The Churches remain wholly free in the action which, on the basis of their convictions and in the light of their ecumenical contacts, they will or will not take.

A very real unity has been discovered in ecumenical meetings which is, to all who collaborate in the World Council, the most precious element of its life. It exists and we receive it again and again as an unmerited gift from the Lord. We praise God for this foretaste of the unity of

His People and continue hopefully with the work to which He has called us together. For the Council exists to serve the Churches as they prepare to meet their Lord Who knows only one flock.

[Lukas Vischer, *A Documentary History of the Faith and Order Movement, 1927-1963*. Copyright and used by permission of the World Council of Churches. Pp. 167-76. See also *Minutes and Reports of the Third Meeting of the Central Committee of the World Council of Churches held at Toronto, Canada, July 9-15, 1950* (Geneva, Switzerland: World Council of Churches, 1950), pp. 84-90.]

North American Conference
on Faith and Order

"The Table of the Lord"

1. At the table of the Lord the Church remembers in thanksgiving and gratitude the life, death and resurrection of Jesus Christ (I Cor. 11:24). What is meant by this commemoration is more than mere recollection of a past event. Our agreement is based on a fresh understanding of the biblical doctrine of God and history. The God of the Bible has not only acted decisively in the past through Christ's atoning death and resurrection; he continues to act in the present; he will continue to act in the future. Therefore, the faithful commemoration of what Christ has done for us is at the same time an action in which Christ mediates himself to us in the present moment. This is the same Christ who will in the last day share with his church the victorious completion of his purpose (Heb. 13:8).

2. Jesus Christ on the night in which he was betrayed chose bread and wine as the elements for the first Eucharist at the Last Supper. Rejecting any one-sided preoccupation with the elements in isolation, we agree that in the entire eucharistic action the whole Christ is personally present as both subject and object, i.e., as the One who is at the same time the Giver and the Gift.

3. In view of our belief in Christ's active presence in the whole eucharistic action, we agree that this action is our participation in his risen life and the fulfillment of his promise to his church.

4. Christ's presence at his table follows from his promise and command. It is only in repentance and faith that the believer as an "empty vessel" receives the fruits of redemption, including the forgiveness of sins, justification, sanctification, newness of life and communion with his brethren. The Holy Spirit bears witness in the present to the reality of these fruits and directs our hope to their realization in the consummation of God's purpose (Romans 8:16-17). The Holy Communion is a means of placing us in the presence of Christ in a total way. In his presence we are judged as well as forgiven (1 Cor. 11:17-34).

5. The indispensable quality of the Eucharist derives from the once-for-all character of the atoning death and resurrection of Jesus Christ as it was prophetically and proleptically set forth in the Last Supper and remembered by and represented in the Christian community. "This do in remembrance of me" (1 Cor. 11:24-25; cf. Luke 22:19) calls us to the table where he has covenanted to meet us. As a consequence of our meeting him at his table we are made aware that he confronts us in other situations where we must respond in faith and love.

6. The Eucharist is therefore in the center of the response of the worshiping church to God's gracious activity in Christ. That which is offered and received in the Eucharist is central to the Christian life. It is important that all elements of proclamation—worship, service, obedience, and mission—be understood in their unity (2 Cor.

9:12-13). Liturgy in the narrow sense is not enough; the service of God by his people in their witness in the world and in winning others to Christ is inextricably bound up with their eucharistic life. The preached word of God is not to be set over against the Supper of the Lord. Both are commanded by Christ; both are involved in his work of redemption.

7. There is a growing realization of the eschatological nature of the Eucharist. "You proclaim the Lord's death until he comes" (1 Cor. 11:26) points unmistakably to the relation between the Supper and the Parousia. Our communion with Christ at the table of the Lord is thus both a present participation in his risen life (1 Cor. 10:16) and a foretaste of the messianic Feast (Mark 14:25; Rev. 19:7-9).

8. In the Eucharist God's covenant with man is renewed as revealed and sealed in Jesus' sacrificial surrender of his life to God and for man. It points continually both to the constancy of God's faithfulness to his covenant people and to the relationship maintained by the renewal of the life of faithful obedience through the power of the Holy Spirit. The new age has broken through; God in Christ makes all things new. It is to this covenant life that we, as heirs of God and joint heirs with Christ (Rom. 8:17) are called and come in the Holy Communion. We are "a royal priesthood, a holy nation" (1 Peter 2:9), called to offer to God our sacrifice of praise and thanksgiving, ourselves, our souls and bodies. By personal participation in the body and blood of the One Lord Jesus Christ, we are strengthened for life in the corporate community of the new covenant and enabled to discern our oneness with

each other. The blessings we receive at the Lord's table empower us for our witness and work in the world into which we are sent.

[Paul S. Minear (ed.), *The Nature of the Unity We Seek* (St. Louis, Mo.: The Bethany Press, 1958), pp. 202-03.]

Third Assembly,
World Council of Churches

"The Church's Unity"

1. The love of the Father and the Son in the unity of the Holy Spirit is the source and goal of the unity which the Triune God wills for all men and creation. We believe that we share in this unity in the Church of Jesus Christ, who is before all things and in whom all things hold together. In him alone, given by the Father to be Head of the Body, the Church has its true unity. The reality of this unity was manifest at Pentecost in the gift of the Holy Spirit, through whom we know in this present age the first fruits of that perfect union of the Son with his Father, which will be known in its fullness only when all things are consummated by Christ in his glory. The Lord who is bringing all things into full unity at the last is he who constrains us to seek the unity which he wills for his Church on earth here and now.

2. We believe that the unity which is both God's will and his gift to his Church is being made visible as all in each place who are baptized into Jesus Christ and confess him as Lord and Saviour are brought by the Holy Spirit into one fully committed fellowship, holding the one apostolic faith, preaching the one Gospel, breaking the one bread, joining in common prayer, and having a

corporate life reaching out in witness and service to all and who at the same time are united with the whole Christian fellowship in all places and all ages in such wise that ministry and members are accepted by all, and that all can act and speak together as occasion requires for the tasks to which God calls his people.

It is for such unity that we believe we must pray and work.

3. This brief description of our objective leaves many questions unanswered. We are not yet of a common mind on the interpretation and the means of achieving the goal we have described. We are clear that unity does not imply simple uniformity of organization, rite or expression. We all confess that sinful self-will operates to keep us separated and that in our human ignorance we cannot discern clearly the lines of God's design for the future. But it is our firm hope that through the Holy Spirit God's will as it is witnessed to in Holy Scripture will be more and more disclosed to us and in us. The achievement of unity will involve nothing less than a death and rebirth of many forms of church life as we have known them. We believe that nothing less costly can finally suffice.

A Commentary upon this Picture of Unity

4. The foregoing paragraph must be understood as a brief description of the sort of unity which would correspond to God's gift and our task. It is not intended as a definition of the Church and it does not presuppose any one particular doctrine of the Church. It is based upon a statement worked out by the Commission on Faith and Order, accepted by the Central Committee at St. Andrews in 1960 and sent to the member churches for considera-

tion and comment. The "Toronto Statement"[1] was a landmark in the World Council's thinking about itself and its relation to work for unity. Here we seek to carry that thought a stage further, not by dictating to the churches their conception of unity but by suggesting for further study an attempt to express more clearly the nature of our common goal. Christian unity has been the primary concern of the Faith and Order movement from the beginning, and the vision of the one Church has become the inspiration of our ecumenical endeavour. We re-affirm that we must go forward to seek the full implications of this vision. We present this statement in the hope that the churches both inside and outside the World Council of Churches will study it with care, and, should it be found inadequate, will formulate alternative statements, which more fully comprehend "both God's will and his gift."

In him alone . . . the Church has its true unity

5. It is in Jesus Christ, God's Son and our only Mediator, that we have union with God. It is he who has given this gift to us through his coming into our world. Unity is not of our making, but as we receive the grace of Jesus Christ we are one in him. We are called to bear witness to the gift of unity through offering our lives as sacrifices to his glory. The fact that we are living in division shows that we have not realized God's gift of unity and we acknowledge our disobedience before him. Our union with God is a mystery which passes our understanding and defeats our efforts to express it adequately. But as Christ has come visibly into this world and has redeemed men of flesh and blood, this union must find visible expression.

[1] *The Church, the Churches and the World Council of Churches,* statement received by the Central Committee at Toronto, 1950.

6. It is the living Christ who impels us to work and pray for a fuller manifestation among us of "the one hope which belongs to our calling." Thus the Faith and Order movement has found the focal point of its study in the person and work of Jesus Christ. Through its Commission on Christ and the Church it has sought to explore the biblical and historical witnesses to Christ, to determine what unity in the one Lord actually means. The unity which is given is the unity of the one Triune God from whom and through whom and to whom are all things. It is the unity which he gives to his people through his decision to dwell among them and to be their God. It is the unity which he gives to his people through the gift of his Son, who by his death and resurrection binds us together in him in his Sonship to the one Father. It is the unity given to his people through his Spirit, and through all the gifts of the Spirit which enliven, edify and empower the new humanity in Christ.

All in each place

7. This statement uses the word "place" both in its primary sense of local neighbourhood and also, under modern conditions, of other areas in which Christians need to express unity in Christ. Thus being one in Christ means that unity among Christians must be found in each school where they study, in each factory or office where they work and in each congregation where they worship, as well as between congregations. "Place" may further imply not only local communities but also wider geographical areas such as states, provinces or nations, and certainly refers to all Christian people in each place regardless of race and class.

Who are baptized into Christ

8. The mutual recognition of baptism, in one sense or another, has been a foundation stone in the ecumenical discussions of the present century. However, closer examination of the assumptions and implications of this fact invariably brings to light deep and wide divergences in theory and practice amongst the churches of the World Council of Churches. Much progress has already been made through the studies of Faith and Order in the understanding of the one baptism.[1] We would urge that these studies be widely circulated among the churches and that the churches in each place study the meaning of baptism together, and in the light of such studies seek to come to a deeper understanding of the baptism by which all have been sealed into the one Lord through their one faith and the gift of the Holy Spirit.

By the Holy Spirit

9. The Church exists in time and place by the power of the Holy Spirit, who effects in her life all the elements that belong to her unity, witness and service. He is the gift of the Father in the name of Jesus Christ to build up the Church, to lead her into the freedom and fellowship which belong to her peace and joy. For any achievement of a fuller unity than that now manifest, we are wholly dependent upon the Spirit's presence and governance.

Fully committed fellowship

10. The word "fellowship" (*koinonia*) has been chosen

[1] "Conference on the Nature of the Unity we Seek" at Oberlin USA, 1957, and in the Report *One Lord, One Baptism*, SCM Press and Augsburg Publishing House, 1960.

because it describes what the Church truly is. "Fellow-ship" clearly implies that the Church is not merely an institution or organization. It is a fellowship of those who are called together by the Holy Spirit and in baptism confess Christ as Lord and Saviour. They are thus "fully committed" to him and to one another. Such a fellowship means for those who participate in it nothing less than a renewed mind and spirit, a full participation in common praise and prayer, the shared realities of penitence and forgiveness, mutuality in suffering and joy, listening together to the same Gospel, responding in faith, obedience and service, joining in the one mission of Christ in the world, a self-forgetting love for all for whom Christ died, and the reconciling grace which breaks down every wall of race, colour, caste, tribe, sex, class and nation. Neither does this "fellowship" imply a rigid uniformity of structure, organization or government. A lively variety marks corporate life in the one Body of one Spirit.

The one apostolic faith

11. The Holy Scriptures of the Old and New Testaments witness to the apostolic faith. This is nothing else than those events which constitute God's call of a people to be his people. The heart of the Gospel (*kerygma*) is Jesus Christ himself, his life and teaching, his death, resurrection, coming (*parousia*) and the justification and sanctification which he brings and offers to all men. The Creeds of the Church witness to this apostolic faith. There are important studies now being undertaken of the relationship between Scripture and Tradition (which is Christian confession down the ages), and attention is drawn to

the work of Faith and Order's Theological Commission on Tradition and Traditions.[1]

Preaching the one Gospel

12. Preaching proclaims anew to men in each generation the Gospel of our Lord Jesus Christ. In the faithful preaching of the Word the living Christ is present as our contemporary in every age; he grants us his grace, he comforts us and calls us to a renewed decision for him. In the human words of the preacher every new generation is confronted by the Christ as one who speaks to them where they actually are.

Breaking the one bread

13. Nowhere are the divisions of our churches more clearly evident and painful than at the Lord's Table. But the Lord's Table is one, not many. In humility the churches must seek that one Table. We would urge the Commission on Faith and Order to continue study and consultation to help us identify and remove those barriers which now keep us from partaking together of the one bread and sharing the one cup.

Joining in common prayer

14. God is to be praised in every tongue and in the setting of every culture and age in an inexhaustible diversity of expression. Yet there are certain common factors in Christian worship such as adoration, penitence, intercession, petition and thanksgiving which are grounded inevitably in the unique acts of God in Christ, discernible still in our divided traditions. As we learn more of each

[1] *The Old and the New in the Church*, SCM Press and Augsburg Publishing House, 1961.

other, we shall more clearly discern this common heritage
and express it more fully.

A corporate life reaching out

15. Mission and service belong to the whole Church.
God calls the Church to go out into the world to witness
and serve in word and deed to the one Lord Jesus Christ,
who loved the world and gave himself for the world. In
the fulfilment of our missionary obedience the call to unity
is seen to be imperative, the vision of one Church pro-
claiming one Gospel to the whole world becomes more
vivid and the experience and expression of our given unity
more real. There is an inescapable relation between the
fulfilment of the Church's missionary obligation and the
recovery of her visible unity.

Ministry and members accepted by all

16. All agree that the whole Body is a royal priesthood.
Yet one of the most serious barriers to unity is our diverse
understanding of the nature of the ministry within the
corporate priesthood. All who have been engaged in
church union negotiations testify to this fact. There are
those, for example, who affirm the necessity of an epis-
copally ordained ministry in the apostolic succession while
others deny that it is essential for the true Church. How
can two such divergent positions on so important a matter
be settled? In this, as in all matters relating to Christ's
Church, it is upon the Holy Spirit we must rely. He will,
if we faithfully search, reveal to us the ways in which we
can have a ministry accepted by all. Here biblical, theological and historical studies must be continued to seek to
lay before the churches that which is necessary to have a

true ministry according to God's Word. The mutual acceptance of members though not so formidable an obstacle as mutual recognition of ministries, still raises problems for some communions. The achievement of a ministry accepted by all would largely resolve the issues involved in the mutual recognition of members.

In all places and all ages
17. Every church and every Christian belongs to Christ. Because we belong to him we are bound through him to the Church and the Christians in all places and all ages. Those who are united in each place are at the same time one with believers in all places. As members of the one Body they share both in each other's joys and sufferings. The Church as a universal fellowship means also that we are part of the People of God of all ages, and as such are one with Abraham, Isaac and Jacob, and all their descendants in the faith until the end of the age. Work for unity in Christ is continually attacked by all the evil forces which fear the light of truth and holiness and obscure our own vision also. We now see our unity only darkly, but we know that then we shall see it clearly when we see him face to face. But it is also our hope which gives us courage to expose our differences and our divisions and call upon God to reveal to us even now that which has hitherto been hidden from our eyes. We pray, with the praying Christ, that *all* may be one. To this end we must work while it is day.

[*The New Delhi Report, The Third Assembly of the World Council of Churches, 1961* (New York: Association Press, 1962), pp. 116-22.]

On Ecumenism,
Chapter III, Part 2

"The Separated Churches and Ecclesial
Communities in the West"

19. The Churches and ecclesial communities which were separated from the Apostolic See of Rome during the grave crisis beginning in the West at the end of the Middle Ages, or in later times, are bound to the Catholic Church by a specially close relationship as a result of the long span of earlier centuries when the Christian people had lived in ecclesiastical communion.

But since these Churches and ecclesial Communities differ considerably not only from us, but also among themselves, due to their different origins and convictions in doctrine and spiritual life, the task of describing them adequately is extremely difficult. We do not propose to do it here.

Although the ecumenical movement and the desire for peace with the Catholic Church have not yet taken hold everywhere, it is nevertheless our hope that the ecumenical spirit and mutual esteem will gradually increase among all men.

At the same time, however, one should recognize that between these Churches and ecclesial Communities on the one hand, and the Catholic Church on the other, there are very weighty differences not only of an historical, sociological, psychological and cultural character, but especially in the interpretation of revealed truth. To facilitate entering into the ecumenical dialogue in spite of those differences, we wish to set down in what follows some considerations which can, and indeed should, serve as a basis and encouragement for such dialogue.

20. Our thoughts are concerned first of all with those Christians who openly confess Jesus Christ as God and Lord and as the only mediator between God and man for the glory of the one God, the Father, the Son and the Holy Spirit. We are indeed aware that there exist considerable differences from the doctrine of the Catholic Church even concerning Christ the Word of God made flesh and the work of redemption, and thus concerning the mystery and ministry of the Church and the role of Mary in the work of salvation. But we rejoice that our separated brethren look to Christ as the source and centre of ecclesiastical communion. Their longing for union with Christ impels them ever more to seek unity, and also to bear witness to their faith among the peoples of the earth.

21. A love and reverence—almost a cult—of Holy Scripture leads our brethren to a constant and diligent study of the sacred text. For the Gospel "is the power of God for salvation to everyone who has faith, to the Jew first and then to the Greek" (Rom. 1:16).

While invoking the Holy Spirit, they seek in these very Scriptures God as He speaks to them in Christ, the One whom the prophets foretold, the Word of God made flesh for us. In the Scriptures they contemplate the life of Christ, as well as the teachings and the actions of the Divine Master for the salvation of men, in particular the mysteries of His death and resurrection.

But when Christians separated from us affirm the divine authority of the Sacred Books, they think differently from us—different ones in different ways—about the relationship between the Scriptures and the Church. For in the Church, according to Catholic belief, its authentic teaching office has a special place in expounding and preaching the written Word of God.

Nevertheless, in the dialogue itself, the Sacred Word is a precious instrument in the mighty hand of God for attaining to that unity which the Saviour holds out to all men.

22. By the Sacrament of baptism, whenever it is properly conferred in the way the Lord determined and received with the proper dispositions of soul, man becomes truly incorporated into the crucified and glorified Christ and is reborn to a sharing of the divine life, as the Apostle says: "For you were buried together with Him in baptism, and in Him also rose again through faith in the working of God who raised Him from the dead (Col. 2:12).[28]

Baptism, therefore, constitutes the sacramental bond of unity existing among all who through it are reborn. But baptism, of itself, is only a beginning, a point of departure, for it is wholly directed toward the acquiring of fullness of life in Christ. Baptism is thus ordained toward a complete profession of faith, a complete incorporation into the system of salvation such as Christ Himself willed it to be, and finally, toward a complete integration into eucharistic communion.

Although the ecclesial Communities separated from us lack the fullness of unity with us which flows from baptism, and although we believe they have not preserved the

[28]Cf. Rom. 6: 4.

proper reality of the eucharistic mystery in its fullness,
especially because of the absence of the sacrament of
Orders, nevertheless when they commemorate the Lord's
death and resurrection in the Holy Supper, they profess
that it signifies life in communion with Christ and await
His coming in glory. For these reasons, the doctrine about
the Lord's Supper, about the other sacraments, worship,
and ministry in the Church, should form subjects of
dialogue.

23. The Christian way of life of these brethren is nour-
ished by faith in Christ. It is strengthened by the grace
of baptism and the hearing of the Word of God. This way
of life expresses itself in private prayer, in meditation of
the Scriptures, in the life of a Christian family, and in the
worship of the community gathered together to praise God.
Furthermore, their worship sometimes displays notable
features of a liturgy once shared in common.

The faith by which they believe in Christ bears fruit in
praise and thanksgiving for the benefits received from the
hands of God. Joined to it is a lively sense of justice and
a true charity towards others. This active faith has been
responsible for many organizations for the relief of spiritual and material distress, the furtherance of education of
youth, the improvement of social conditions of life, and the
promotion of peace throughout the world.

And if in moral matters there are many Christians who
do not always understand the Gospel in the same way as
Catholics, and do not admit the same solutions for the
more difficult problems of modern society, they nevertheless want to cling to Christ's word as the source of Christian virtue and to obey the command of the Apostle:
"Whatever you do in word or in work, do all in the name

of the Lord Jesus, giving thanks to God the Father through him" (Col. 3:17). Hence, the ecumenical dialogue could start with the moral application of the Gospel.

24. Now, after this brief exposition of the conditions under which ecumenical activity may be practiced, and of the principles by which it is to be guided, we confidently look to the future. This sacred Council urges the faithful to abstain from any frivolousness or imprudent zeal, for these can cause harm to true progress towards unity. Their ecumenical activity cannot be other than fully and sincerely catholic, that is, loyal to the truth we have received from the Apostles and the Fathers, and in harmony with the faith which the Catholic Church has always professed, and at the same time tending towards that fullness in which Our Lord wants His Body to grow in the course of time.

This sacred Council firmly hopes that the initiatives of the sons of the Catholic Church joined with those of the separated brethren will go forward, without obstructing the ways of divine Providence, and without prejudging the future inspiration of the Holy Spirit. Further, this Council declares that it realizes that this holy objective—the reconciliation of all Christians in the unity of the one and only Church of Christ—transcends human powers and gifts. It therefore places its hope entirely in the prayer of Christ for the Church, in the love of the Father for us, and in the power of the Holy Spirit. "And hope does not disappoint, because God's love has been poured forth in our hearts through the Holy Spirit who has been given to us" (Rom. 5:5).

[Vatican II (1962-1966), *Decree On Ecumenism,* Promulgated Nov. 21, 1964

(Rome: Typis Polyglottis Vaticanis, 1965), Chap. III, Part 2, pars. 19-24. Cf. Vatican II, *The Decree on Ecumenism,* trans. The Secretariat for Promoting Christian Unity (New York: Paulist Press, 1965).]

BOOKS ON ECUMENICITY

Books marked with an asterisk (*) are particularly recommended. Books in print may be
ordered from the Cokesbury Book Store serving your territory. Prices are subject to change.
Books available from the World Council of
Churches, 475 Riverside Drive, New York, N.Y.
10027, are indicated with a †.

†ABRECHT, PAUL. *The Churches and Rapid Social
Change.* Garden City, N.Y.: Doubleday & Co., 1961.
Out-of-print. London: S. C. M. Press, 1961. $3.95.

ADAM, KARL. *The Spirit of Catholicism,* trans. by
Justin McCann. Garden City, N.Y.: Doubleday &
Co., 1959. Paper, 85 cents. (DD)

BAYNE, STEPHEN F., JR. *Ceylon, North India, Pakistan:
Study in Ecumenical Discussion.* Greenwich, Conn.:
Seabury Press, 1960. Paper, $2.25. (SN)

*BEA, AUGUSTINE CARDINAL. *The Unity of Christians.*
New York: Herder Book Center, 1963. $4.95.

*BEAVER, R. PIERCE. *Ecumenical Beginnings in Protes-
tant World Mission: A History of Comity.* New
York: Thos. Nelson & Sons, 1962. $5.00. (TN)

*BELL, GEORGE K. A., ed. *Documents on Christian Unity:
A Selection from the First and Second Series, 1920-
1930.* New York: Oxford University Press, 1955.
Out-of-print.

BELL, GEORGE K. A., ed. *Documents on Christian Unity,
4th Series, 1948-1957.* New York: Oxford University Press, 1958. $3.40 (OU)

†BRIDSTON, KEITH R. and WAGONER, WALTER D. *Unity
in Mid-Career—An Ecumenical Critique.* New York:
Macmillan Co., 1963. Out-of-print. $4.95.

*BROWN, ROBERT MCAFEE and WEIGEL, GUSTAVE, S. J., *An American Dialogue*. Garden City, N.Y.: Doubleday & Co., 1960. Paper, 95 cents. (DD)

BROWN, ROBERT MCAFEE and SCOTT, DAVID H., eds. *The Challenge to Reunion: The Blake Proposal Under Scrutiny.* New York: McGraw-Hill Book Co., 1963. $6.50. (MH)

*BROWN, ROBERT MCAFEE. *The Spirit of Protestantism.* New York: Oxford University Press, 1961. $5.00. Trade Ed. (OU)

*BROWN, WILLIAM ADAMS. *Toward a United Church: Three Decades of Ecumenical Christianity.* New York: Chas. Scribner's Sons, 1946. Out-of-print.

*CARTER, HENRY. *The Methodist Heritage.* Nashville: Abingdon Press, 1952. $4.25. (AP)

CATE, WILLIAM B. *The Ecumenical Scandal on Main Street.* New York: Association Press, 1965. $3.50. (AY)

†*CAVERT, S. M. *On the Road to Christian Unity.* New York: Harper & Bros., 1961. Out-of-print. $3.75.

COBB, JOHN B., JR. *Varieties of Protestantism.* Philadelphia: Westminster Press, 1960. Out-of-print.

Conversations Between the Church of England and the Methodist Church, Interim Statement. Naperville, Ill.: Alec R. Allenson, 1958. Out-of-print.

Conversations Between the Church of England and the Methodist Church. Naperville, Ill.: Alec R. Allenson, 1963. $1.25. (AA)

†CROW, PAUL A., JR. *The Ecumenical Movement in Bibliographical Outline.* New York: Department of Faith and Order, The National Council of the Churches of Christ in the U.S.A., 1965. $2.00.

Digest of the Proceedings of the Consultation on Church Union for 1962 (Washington, D.C.) and 1963 (Oberlin, Ohio). Volumes I and II combined. $2.00. *The Consultation on Church Union, Princeton, New*

Jersey, April, 1964. Vol. III. $2.00. *Digest of the Proceedings of the Fourth Meeting of the Consultation on Church Union, Lexington, Kentucky, 1965.* Vol. IV. $3.00. Available from Consultation on Church Union, Rev. George L. Hunt, Executive Secretary, Box 69, Fanwood, N.J. 07023.

DOUGLASS, HARLAN PAUL. *Church Unity Movements in the United States.* New York: Institute of Social and Religious Research, 1934. Out-of-print.

†*Ecumenical Review, The* (bound files) 1948--. W. A. Visser't Hooft, ed. Geneva: World Council of Churches. 4 issues of about 128 pages a year, $4.00. Single copy, $1.25.

*EHRENSTROM, NILS and MUELDER, WALTER G., eds. *Institutionalism and Church Unity.* New York: Association Press, 1963. $6.50. (AY)

*FLETCHER, GRACE N. *The Whole World's in His Hand.* Illustrated. New York: E. P. Dutton & Co., 1962. $4.50. (DU)

FLEW, R. NEWTON. *The Catholicity of Protestantism.* Philadelphia: Fortress Press, 1950. Out-of-print.

GERRISH, B. A., ed. *The Faith of Christendom*: *A Sourcebook of Creeds and Confessions.* Cleveland, Ohio: World Publishing Co., 1963. Paper, $1.95. (WD)

GOODALL, NORMAN. *The Ecumenical Movement*: *What It is and What It Does.* 2nd ed. New York: Oxford University Press, 1964. $5.00. (OU)

GRANT, FREDERICK C. *Rome and Reunion.* New York: Oxford University Press, 1965. $5.00. (OU)

†*HOGG, W. RICHEY. *Ecumenical Foundations* (International Missionary Council). New York: Harper & Bros., 1952. Out-of-print. $1.95.

HOGG, W. RICHEY. *Tomorrow Is Here.* New York: Friendship Press, 1948. Out-of-print.

HOLT, IVAN LEE and CLARK, ELMER T. *The World Methodist Movement*. Nashville: The Upper Room, 1956. Out-of-print.

†HUNT, GEORGE L. *A Guide to Christian Unity*. Rev. ed. St. Louis, Mo.: The Bethany Press, 1963. Paper, $1.25. (CB)

Jersualem Meeting Report (Conference of the International Missionary Council, 1928). London: Oxford University Press, 1928. 8 vol. Out-of-print.

> *The Christian Life and Message in Relation to Non-Christian Systems of Thought and Life,* Vol. I
> *Religious Education,* Vol. II
> *The Younger and Older Churches,* Vol. III
> *Mission and Race Conflict,* Vol. IV
> *Mission and Industrialism,* Vol. V
> *Mission and Rural Problems,* Vol. VI
> *International Missionary Operation,* Vol. VII
> *Addresses and Other Records,* Vol. VIII

KENNEDY, JAMES W. *COCU* [Consultation on Church Union]. Cincinnati: Forward Movement Publications, 1965. 25 cents.

KENNEDY, JAMES W. *Evanston Notebook* (Comments on Second Assembly of World Council of Churches). New York: Committee on Interpretation and Support, U. S. Conference of the World Council of Churches, 1954. Out-of-print.

†KENNEDY, JAMES W. *Evanston Scrapbook* (An account of the Second Assembly of the World Council of Churches). Lebanon, Pa.: Sowers Printing Co., 1954. 50 cents.

†KENNEDY, JAMES W. *No Darkness at All*. St. Louis: The Bethany Press, 1962. Paper, $1.50. (CB)

*KIK, J. MARCELLUS. *Ecumenism and the Evangelical*. Nutley, N.J.: Presbyterian and Reformed Publishing Co., 1958. $2.50.

*KÜNG, HANS. *The Council, Reform, and Reunion.* New York: Sheed and Ward, 1962. $3.95.

†*LAMPE, G. W. H. and PATON, DAVID M., eds. *The Old and the New in the Church: Studies in Ministry and Worship.* Minneapolis, Minn.: Augsburg Publishing House, 1962. Paper, $1.25. (AU)

*LEE, ROBERT. *The Social Sources of Church Unity.* New York: Abingdon Press, 1960. $4.50. (AP)

*LEITH, JOHN H., ed. *Creeds of the Churches.* Garden City, N. Y.: Doubleday & Co., 1963. Paper, $1.95. (DD) .

MACKAY, JOHN A. *Ecumenics: the Science of the Church Universal.* New York: Prentice-Hall, 1964. $5.95. (PH)

MCNEILL, JOHN T. *Unitive Protestantism: The Ecumenical Spirit and its Persistent Expression.* Rev. ed. Richmond, Va.: John Knox Press, 1964. $4.50. (JK)

The Madras Series (Conference of the International Missionary Council, Tambaram, Madras, India, 1938), 7 vols. New York: International Missionary Council, 1939. Out-of-print.

> *The Authority of the Faith,* Vol. I
> *The Growing Church,* Vol. II
> *Evangelism,* Vol. III
> *The Life of the Church,* Vol. IV
> *The Economic Basis of the Church,* Vol. V
> *The Church and the State,* Vol. VI
> *Addresses and Other Records,* Vol. VII

MARSHALL, ROMNEY P. and TAYLOR, M. J. *Liturgy and Christian Unity.* Englewood Cliffs, N.J.: Prentice-Hall, 1965. $4.95. (PH)

*MARTY, MARTIN E. *Church Unity and Church Mission.* Grand Rapids, Mich.: Wm. B. Eerdmans Co., 1964. $3.00. (EP)

186

MILLER, J. QUINTER. *Christian Unity: Its Relevance to the Community*. Strausburg, Va.: Shenandoah Press, 1957. Out-of-print.

MINEAR, PAUL S. *The Images of the Church in the New Testament*. Philadelphia: Westminster Press, 1960. $6.00. (WP)

†MINEAR, PAUL S., ed. *Faith and Order Findings* (The Final Report of the Theological Commission to the Fourth World Conference on Faith and Order, Montreal, 1963). Minneapolis: Augsburg Publishing House, 1963. Out-of-print. $4.50.

MOLLAND, EINAR. *Christendom*. London: A. R. Mowbray & Co., Ltd., 28 Margaret St., W. 1, England, 1959 (available by special order). $10.00.

*MOORE, JOHN M. *The Long Road to Methodist Union*. Nashville: Abingdon Press, 1958. $3.00. (AP) (See also Joseph L. Allen, "The Methodist Union in the U.S.," *Institutionalism and Church Unity*, ed. by Nils Ehrenstrom and Walter G. Muelder).

National Council Outlook. Journal of Interdenominational Cooperation (Jan., 1951—June, 1959 bound files); New York: National Council of Churches. Ceased.

†NELSON, J. ROBERT, ed. *Christian Unity in North America*. St. Louis, Mo.: Bethany Press, 1958. $1.75. (CB)

†NELSON, J. ROBERT. *Overcoming Christian Divisions*. New York: Association Press, 1962. Paper, 75 cents. (AY)

NEWBIGIN, LESSLIE. *A Faith for This One World*. New York: Harper & Row, 1962. Out-of-print.

NEWBIGIN, LESSLIE. *The Household of God*. New York: Friendship Press, 1954. Paper, $2.25. (MM)

*NEWBIGIN, LESSLIE. *The Reunion of the Church*. Rev. ed. Naperville, Ill.: Alec R. Allenson, 1960. Out-of-print.

*NIEBUHR, H. RICHARD. *The Social Sources of Denominationalism*. Gloucester, Mass.: Peter Smith, Publisher, n.d. $3.50.

†ORR, GRACE DOUGLAS. *Layman's Guide to Ecumenicity*. New York: World Council of Churches, 1956. 75 cents.

OSBORN, RONALD E. *A Church for These Times*. Nashville: Abingdon Press, 1965. Paper, $1.95. (AP)

*OUTLER, ALBERT C. *The Christian Tradition and the Unity We Seek*. New York: Oxford University Press, 1957. $3.25. (OU)

PIPER, OTTO A. *Protestantism in an Ecumenical Age*. Philadelphia: Fortress Press, 1965. $4.50. (FR)

†RODGER, P. C. and VISCHER, LUKAS. *The Fourth World Conference on Faith and Order, Montreal, 1963*. New York: Association Press, 1964. $3.95. (AY)

*ROUSE, RUTH and NEILL, STEPHEN C. *A History of the Ecumenical Movement, 1517-1948*. Philadelphia: Westminster Press, 1954. Out-of-print.

SANDERSON, ROSS W. *Church Cooperation in the United States*. New York: Association of Council Secretaries, Council of Churches, 60 Lorraine St., Hartford, Conn. 06105, 1960. $1.50.

SCHAFF, PHILIP. *Creeds of Christendom*. New York: Harper & Bros., 1905. Out-of-print.

†*SKOGLUND, JOHN E. and NELSON, J. ROBERT. *Fifty Years of Faith and Order*. New York: World Council of Churches, Committee for ISM, 1963. $1.75.

SKYDSGAARD, K. E. *The Papal Council and the Gospel*. Minneapolis: Augsburg Press, 1961. $3.95. (AU)

STEPHANOU, EUSEBIUS A. *The Orthodox Church and the Ecumenical Movement*. Available at the Holy Cross Theological Book Store, 50 Goddard Ave., Brookline, Mass. 02146. $1.00.

SUNDKLER, BENGT. *The Church of South India: The Movement Toward Union, 1900-47.* London: Lutterworth Press, 1954. $3.50.

SWIDLER, LEONARD, ed. *Scripture and Ecumenism.* New York: Herder Book Center, 1965. $4.95.

*TAVARD, GEORGE H. *Two Centuries of Ecumenism.* Notre Dame, Ind.: Fides Publishers, Inc., 1960. Out-of-print.

VAN DUSEN, HENRY P. *One Great Ground of Hope: Christian Missions and Christian Unity.* Philadelphia: Westminster Press, 1961. Out-of-print.

*VATICAN COUNCIL II, CONSTITUTIONS AND DECREES:
The Constitution on the Sacred Liturgy of the Second Vatican Council with Commentary by Jerard S. Sloyan. New York: Paulist Press, 1964. Pamphlet, 50 cents.
The Constitution on the Church of Vatican Council II. Commentary by Gregory Baum, O.S.A. New York: Paulist Press, 1965. Paper, 95 cents.
The Decree on Ecumenism. New York: Paulist Press, 1965. 50 cents.

†VISCHER, LUKAS, ed. *A Documentary History of the Faith and Order Movement, 1927-1963.* St. Louis, Mo.: The Bethany Press, 1963. Paper, $2.00. (CB)

†*VISSER'T HOOFT, W. A., ed. *First Assembly of the World Council of Churches, The Official Report, Amsterdam, 1948.* New York: Harper & Row, 1949. Out-of-print.

*VISSER'T HOOFT, W. A., ed. *Evanston Report: World Council of Churches, Second Assembly.* New York: Harper & Row, 1955. Out-of-print.

†*VISSER'T HOOFT, W. A., ed. *The New Delhi Report* (Official Report of World Council of Churches: Third Assembly). "New Delhi Story," day-by-day

account by Samuel McCrea Cavert. New York: Association Press, 1962. $6.50. (AY)

*WEBBER, GEORGE W. *God's Colony in Man's World.* Nashville: Abingdon Press, 1960. $2.75. (AP)

WEDEL, THEODORE. *The Coming Great Church: Essays on Church Unity.* New York: The Macmillan Co., 1945. Out-of-print.

*WEIGEL, GUSTAVE. *Catholic Theology in Dialogue.* New York: Harper & Row, 1961. Out-of-print.

WOLF, WILLIAM J., ed. *Protestant Churches and Reform Today.* Greenwich, Conn.: Seabury Press, 1964. $3.95. (SN)

†*WORLD COUNCIL OF CHURCHES; SECOND ASSEMBLY (preparatory material). *The Christian Hope and the Task of the Church.* New York: Harper & Row, 1954. Out-of-print. $5.00.

GLOSSARY

[This Glossary has been prepared by the editors for the convenience of those who may find it of use.]

AD INTERIM—in the meantime.

AGGREGATION—collection into a mass or sum; a number of people; collection into an unorganized whole.

AMBIVALENCE—opposite or conflicting feelings or attitudes about the same plan, person, or thing.

ANOMALY—something incongruous or abnormal; deviation from a logical conclusion.

APOSTASY—the abandonment or renunciation of a religious faith.

APOSTOLICITY—historical continuity with the first apostles and the early Christian community.

BIGOTRY—obstinate or unreasoning attachment to one's own belief or opinion; intolerance of differing beliefs.

CANARD—a false or unfounded story or report; a groundless belief.

CATHOLIC—the Roman Catholic, Eastern Orthodox, and Anglican churches as contrasted with the Protestants; also, universal, all-inclusive.

CLERUS—Latin for clergy; from the Greek *klerks*.

COLLEGIAL—relating to a collegium or group of associates.

COLLEGIUM—a corporate body in which all members share collective authority.

CONCILIAR—relating to or issued by a council.

CONCILIARISM—the theory of church government that places final ecclesiastical authority in representative church councils.

CONFIRMANDS—candidates for confirmation or full membership in the church.

CONFIRMATION—a rite of some Christian churches regarded as supplemental to the rite of baptism, held by some churches to be a sacrament, and viewed generally as confirming a person in his Christian faith.

CONGERIES—a collection of things merely heaped together; a jumble of people, things, or ideas.

COROLLARY—a proposition that follows upon another just demonstrated and requiring no additional proof; a deduction, consequence, or additional inference.

COTERIE—a small group of persons having a common interest or purpose, or following a particular leader or cause; an "in"-group.

DE-MYTHOLOGIZE—to change a tale or account from the status of a myth to that of a sign or symbol.

DICHOTOMY—division into two parts; separation into mutually exclusive sections.

DISPARATE—essentially different; connected only by some notion or interest of great generality or extreme catholicity.

DOCETIC—relating to that view of Jesus Christ which saw in him only an "appearance" (*dokesis*) and not a full and real historical person. Thus, he only "appeared" to suffer and to die.

DOCTRINAIRE—arbitrary; insisting upon the application of a theory or doctrine without regard to its practical consequences.

DONATISTS—a group of North African Christians in the fourth and fifth centuries who opposed the Catholic party because of a controversy over the character and validity of Catholic ordination. Engaged by St. Augustine in a famous controversy over the nature of the church, the ministry, and the sacraments, in which St. Augustine advocated their repression by the civil power.

ECUMENISM—the study of the nature, mission, problems, and strategy of the Christian church from the perspective of its character as a worldwide Christian fellowship, often including within its scope an emphasis on the contributions of Christian mission work to the rise of a movement toward union between the churches; a concern for the recomposition of Christian unity.

ECUMENICAL—general, pertaining to the whole Christian church.

EPISCOPATE—the body of bishops; the office of a bishop.

ESCHATOLOGY—the doctrine of the last or final things, death, resurrection, the second coming of Christ; ESCHATOLOGICAL—relating to the judgment, the future state, the ultimate destiny of mankind and the world.

ETHOS—atmosphere; underlying spirit and character of a community or people; the spirit which produces and actuates manners and customs, especially moral attitudes.

FILIOQUE—"and the Son," the term added to the Nicene Creed in the West in the seventh century. The Orthodox objected both to the innovation as such and also to its doctrinal implications. This issue became one of the chief causes of the eventual split between Rome and Constantinople (A.D. 1054).

INCARNATION—the union of divinity with humanity; specifically, in Christianity, the revelation of God in Jesus Christ.

INDIFFERENTISM—the principle or conviction that differences in religious beliefs are essentially unimportant.

INTERNECINE—mutually destructive; involving conflict to the death within a group.

KALEIDOSCOPIC—successively changing in views, phases, or actions.

KERYGMA—the original Christian gospel preached by the apostles.

KOINONIA—intimate spiritual communion; fellowship in a common religious commitment and spiritual community.

LATITUDINARIANISM—the view that differences in church order, polity, and ritual may be very wide (*latus,* broad) and still not occasion schism or disunity.

LITURGY—the public worship of God; man's corporate service of God; also, the rituals by which this worship is conducted.

MAGISTERIUM—the church's teaching power or function; in the Roman Catholic Church, the teaching authority of the Pope and the other bishops.

MALINE CONVERSATIONS—from 1921-26 what were known as the Maline Conversations were carried on intermittently between several Anglo-Catholics on the one hand and, on the other, Cardinal Mercier of Belgium and some others of the Roman Catholic Church. They were discontinued after the death of Cardinal Mercier. See *A History of Christianity,* by Kenneth Scott Latourette (New York: Harper & Bros., copyright 1953), p. 1390.

MEDIA—things through or by which something is accomplished, conveyed, or carried on (the plural of medium).

MONOPHYSITE—one who maintains the doctrine that the human and divine in the person of Jesus Christ constitute only one "nature" *(monophysis*—one nature) which is regarded either as thoroughly unified or as composite. They rejected the "two natures" doctrine of the Council of Chalcedon (A.D. 451) and formed separate churches which still persist.

NATURALISM—a doctrine that all truth is derived from nature and not from miraculous or supernatural revelation; thus, a denial of the miraculous or supernatural in religion.

NICENE CREED—the confession of faith formulated and decreed by the Council of Nicaea (A.D. 325) which asserts that Jesus Christ shares the divine essence with God the Father. This was in opposition to Arianism which asserted that the Son of God was a creature of a different essence from the Father.

OECUMENICAL—variation and original spelling of "ecumenical" (based on the Greek word, *oikoumenikos,* meaning "the inhabited world"); pertaining to the whole world or to the church throughout the world; catholic, general, universal.

OMNICOMPETENCE—the ability to act in all matters.

OPT—to choose between two or more options.

ORTHODOX—correct or sound in doctrine or opinion.

ORTHODOX CHURCH—the Eastern or Greek Christian Church.

PAN-DENOMINATIONAL — including all the groups in a given denominational family.

PARACLETE—the Holy Spirit of God (cf. John 14:16, 26; 16:7).

PAROUSIA—the climax of the Christ-Event; His expected "appearance" or "second coming" . . . "to judge both the living and the dead."

PHALANX—a number of persons or groups closely united for a common purpose.

POLEMIC—controversial discussion or argument; theological controversy; the art and practice of disputation.

POLITY—form of government, constitution, or organization of a religious institution.

PRAGMATISTS—those who put emphasis on the application of ideas or the practical bearings of conceptions and beliefs.

PRESBYTERS—the "elders" among the clergy of a church; the highest rank of the ministry in Presbyterian and Methodist churches; the rank below the bishops in the episcopally-ordered churches.

PREVENIENT—anticipatory; PREVENIENT GRACE—divine grace that is said to operate on the human will before it has turned to God.

PROLEPSIS—the representation or assumption of a future act or development as being presently existing or accomplished.

PROLEPTICALLY—in anticipation, as if already on the verge of a significant event.

PROVIDENCE—the power and presence of God in history, sustaining and giving meaning to the events of history and to the destinies of men; PROVIDENTIAL—occurring by or as if by God's Providence.

QUINTESSENTIAL—of highest importance; truly essential.

REMNANT—small group of the faithful; a minority of Israel preserved by God from the calamities visited upon the wicked to become the nucleus of a new and holy community (Isaiah 11:11, 16; 46:1-4).

RITUAL—the prescribed order and words of a religious ceremony; the form for conducting a devotional service.

SACERDOTAL—priestly; relating to the priesthood or the priestly office or function; assuming the necessity of an authorized priesthood as a mediator between men and their divine needs or aspirations.

SACRAL—holy, sacred; relating to the spiritual dimension of life and human culture.

SACROSANCT—most holy or sacred; untouchable.

SCHISM—a split, or disharmony; breach of unity among people of the same religious faith; division or separation in or from a church or religious body; SCHISMATIC—one who separates from a religious body because of a difference in opinion.

SEMPER REFORMANDA—always in process of being reformed.

SUBSTANTIVE—enduring or permanent, real, not merely apparent.

THEOLOGY—critical reflection about God, methodically formulated; the scientifically critical, historical, and psychological study of religion and religious ideas; SYSTEMATIC THEOL-

OGY—the attempt to set forth the major doctrines and teachings of the Christian church in a systematic way, to show the grounds on which they rest, and to make clear their relevance for the human situation.

TRADITION—the process, present in the Bible and in the history of the church, by which beliefs and practices are received from the past and transmitted to the future generations in the church.

TRANSUBSTANTIATION—the change of the Eucharistic elements at their consecration in the Roman Catholic mass from the substance of bread and wine to the substance of the body and blood of Christ with only the "accidents" (as taste, color, shape, smell) of the bread and wine remaining.

UNA SANCTA—the one Holy Church.

UNIATE—a member of one of the churches of Eastern Christendom in communion with Rome which yet retain their respective languages, rites, and canon law in accordance with the terms of their union with Rome.

WORD—the divine Wisdom; the Logos; the Eternal Son of God who became Incarnate in Jesus Christ; the revelation of God in Christ.

Cf.—compare

Ibid.—the same reference

Op. cit.—in the work mentioned earlier

P.—page

Pp.—pages

Seq.—and following

NOTES ON THE COVER

Each person's interpretation of the cover will be colored by his own experience and concern. The cover design is intended to convey the growing unity of Christian churches around the world. The *three forms* of church architecture are not meant to represent any particular churches or religions. Rather, they are intended to symbolize all structures used for the worship of God. The overlapping of these architectural designs indicates the interrelatedness of churches throughout the world.

The *circle* which encloses the churches is symbolic of oneness, unity; it also represents the world. The *spire* breaking through the circle suggests that for God there are no spacial limitations.

The colors of the cover are also symbolic. *White,* symbol of the Creator, light, perfection, and rejoicing, points with sincerity of intent toward the goal of Christian unity —"that all may be one" and "that the world may believe." *Blue-green* symbolizes hope and growth in the Christian life. *Gold* signifies the glory of God, prayer, and the warmth and closeness of all who believe in God.

The two lines from Tennyson on the back cover, beside the golden chain, are from a passage of "Morte d'Arthur" which begins, "More things are wrought by prayer than this world dreams of. . . ."

Mamie Harmon, the artist whose perceptive interpretations in various art forms make her well known both in this country and abroad, is the daughter of a Methodist minister. A writer as well as a designer and painter, Miss Harmon has written on art subjects for such publications as the *Encyclopedia of World Art* and the *Dictionary of Folklore.*

Editor.

THE AUTHOR

ALBERT OUTLER is parsonage born and bred, in Georgia (where his father before him was a Methodist minister for half a century). He was educated at Wofford, Emory, and Yale—and served charges in the South Georgia Conference for seven years. He began teaching theology at Duke in 1938; moved, in 1945, to Yale, where he was Dwight Professor of Theology; then to SMU in 1951, where he has been ever since. He is a past president of the American Theological Society and also of the American Society of Church History. His books include: *Psychotherapy and the Christian Message, St. Augustine's Confessions and Enchiridion* in the "Library of Christian Classics," *The Christian Tradition and the Unity We Seek,* and *John Wesley* in "A Library of Protestant Thought." He is currently engaged in producing a new edition of John Wesley's *Sermons* and a history of the Second Vatican Council.

Professor Outler's ecumenical studies began in his graduate school days at Yale, where he collaborated with Professor R. L. Calhoun in preparation for the Oxford Conference on Life and Work (1937). He has been a Methodist delegate to the World Conferences on Faith and Order at Lund (1952) and Montreal (1963) and to the Third Assembly of the World Council of Churches in New Delhi (1961). A member of the Faith and Order Commission, and of its Working Committee, since 1952, he is also vice-chairman of the Methodist Commission on Ecumenical Affairs (the sub-Commission on Study and Liaison). He is a member of the North Texas Conference.

Professor Outler is married and has a daughter, a son, and a granddaughter. His hobbies are gardening, photography, and "hi-fi."

Editorial and Literature Department
Joint Commission on Education and Cultivation

Order from

SERVICE CENTER
Board of Missions — The Methodist Church
7820 Reading Road, Cincinnati, Ohio 45237
Price, $1.00

FE566

SC-012